Inf[illegible]hnology and Computer Literacy

Students' Book

This book is t

Information Technology and Computer Literacy

Students' Book

Joyce Mount
Lecturer in Office Technology
South Cheshire College

McGRAW-HILL BOOK COMPANY

London . New York . St Louis . San Francisco . Auckland
Bogotá . Caracus . Hamburg . Lisbon . Madrid . Mexico . Milan
Montreal . New Delhi . Panama . Paris . San Juan . São Paulo
Singapore . Sydney . Tokyo . Toronto

Published by
McGRAW-HILL Book Company (UK) Limited
Shoppenhangers Road, Maidenhead, Berkshire, SL6 2QL, England.
Tel 0628 23432
Fax 0628 35895

British Library Cataloguing in Publication Data
Mount, Joyce
Information technology and computer literacy.
Students' book
1. Computer systems
I. Title
004

ISBN 0–07–707277–4

1234 93210
Typeset by Oxprint Ltd, Oxford
and printed and bound in Great Britain by Information Press, Eynsham

To Phil for his help and
encouragement and to my
mother for her perseverance

Contents

Acknowledgements

To the RSA for the use of the Profile Sentences from the CLAIT syllabus

Introduction

This Students' Book is designed to provide an ideal step-wise approach to the subject of Information Technology and Computer Literacy, whether it is being studied in its own right, or as part of a broader course.

Produced in conjunction with a complementary Teacher's Manual and designed to be used with any available software package, the book is divided into eight main sections, the successful completion of which leads ultimately to the award of the Royal Society of Art's CLAIT examination. Aspects covered include word processing, spreadsheets, databases, graphics, stock control, payroll, Viewdata and desktop publishing, whilst additional sections – 'Improve Your Display' and 'Proofreading' – help the student to input data both accurately and attractively.

For ease of use, each section is divided into a series of 'Tasks', where new concepts of Information Technology are introduced. The student is warned in advance of the knowledge required to complete the Tasks. The teacher should ensure that the student understands how to use the software package. An individual manual for the package could be provided by the teacher for use throughout the Tasks and Assignments. Where no warning is given of the concepts in the Task, it is assumed that the knowledge has been acquired on a previous occasion.

Having completed the Tasks, the student is encouraged to embark on a series of 'Assignments', from which his or her progress may be assessed by the teacher. Assignment Progress Sheets are provided in the Teacher's Manual – these can be completed at the end of each assignment with P for Pass or F for Fail (or some kind of indication). The student will only Pass when all sections of the Progress Sheet have been marked P. In the event of greater practice being required, or greater confidence needing to be developed, three additional assignments, together with keys for all the assignments, are available from the accompanying Teacher's Manual. Checklists for revision during and at the end of the course are provided.

1 Word processing

TASK 1 In this task, there are seven simple passages to be keyed in. When these have been saved and printed, the documents are to be recalled and changes made to the margins and/or line spacing. The passages also include simple edit instructions for addition, deletion and replacement of words.

Check

- The spacing between the words.
- The spacing after punctuation.
- The spacing between paragraphs.

Above all, check your display, but remember, be consistent!

?

DO YOU KNOW?

How to set margins?

What spacing to use after punctuation?

What line spacing to use between paragraphs?

How many characters there are in one inch?

How to save a document?

How to print a document?

How to set the printer at 'top of form'?

Data Entry Errors

What is a Data Entry Error?

1 Any character or word which is incorrect, which has been omitted or is additional to the text, or which has been omitted.

2 One error per word only can be counted, eg obi*v*ous*yl* – although there are two errors within the word, they count as one.

3 If an error is repeated it counts once only.

4 If the error is corrected *before* the final printout, it is ignored.

5 *Only three data entry errors are allowed* – check carefully.

Passage 1

Filename: PASS1
Format the document as follows:

set left margin of 1″
set right margin of 0.5″
single line spacing

Key in the following document:

> I enjoy walking in the countryside during the autumn. The air is so clean and crisp and there are so many interesting things to see.
>
> The leaves are beginning to change colour. The colours vary from green through to that beautiful brown, and I often wish I were a painter so that I could capture some of that beauty on canvas. I cannot paint, so I take my camera with me, and try to recapture on film some of the fascinating things which are there around me.
>
> When I go into the woods, I try to discover how many different types of trees I can recognise. Do you know the difference between the trees? If not, take a book along with you and compare your samples with those in the illustrations.

1 Save the document using filename PASS1 and print a copy.

DO YOU KNOW?

How to recall a document?

How to change the left margin of an existing document?

How to change the line spacing of an existing document?

What line spacing to use between paragraphs in double line spacing?

How to delete words from text?

If not, improve your display!

2 Recall document PASS1.

3 Inset the left margin by 1″.

4 Change all the text to double line spacing.

5 Delete the words crossed through in the following passage:

> I enjoy walking in the countryside during the autumn. The air is ~~so~~ clean and crisp and there are so many interesting things to see.
>
> The leaves are beginning to change colour. The colours vary from green ~~through~~ to ~~that~~ beautiful brown, and I ~~often~~ wish I were a painter so that I could capture some of that beauty on canvas. I cannot paint, so I take my camera with me, and try to recapture ~~on film~~ some of the fascinating things which are ~~there~~ around me.
>
> When I go into the woods, I try to discover how many different types of trees I can recognise. Do you know the difference between ~~the~~ trees? If not, take a book along with you and compare your samples with ~~those in~~ the illustrations.

6 Save the file and print a copy.

Passage 2

Filename: PASS2
Format the document as follows:

set left margin of 1″
set right margin of 0.5″
single line spacing

The office of today is different from the office of yesterday. I remember the first office I worked in. The only equipment in sight - my old typewriter and what now seems a very ancient adding machine.

The office belonged to the Treasury of a local authority, and all financial matters were dealt with. The payroll was calculated manually, the invoices were typed by me after the clerk had calculated them on paper or in his head, and the rent and rate records were completed by hand. As there was always a deadline to meet, there was always a panic.

I am sure if I were to return now after 25 years, I would find many differences. The computer will have taken over most, if not all, of the tasks.

1 Save the document using filename PASS2 and print a copy.

DO YOU KNOW?

How to change the line spacing of one paragraph in an existing document?

How to change both margins of one paragraph?

How to change the line spacing of one paragraph?

How to insert words into existing text?

2 Recall document PASS2.

3 Change the margins of the second paragraph by 0.5″ on each side.

4 Change first and third paragraphs to double line spacing.

5 Add the inserted words into the text.

very
The office of today is/different from the office of

yesterday. I remember the first office I worked in.

pieces of manual
The only/equipment in sight - my old/typewriter and

what now seems a very ancient adding machine.

Department
The office belonged to the Treasury/of a local

consequently
authority, and all/financial matters were dealt with.

and handwritten
The payroll was calculated manually/, the invoices

either
were typed by me after the clerk had calculated them/

on paper or in his head, and the rent and rate

```
records were completed by hand.  As there was always
a deadline to meet, there was always a panic.

I am sure if I were to return now after 25 years, I
would find many differences.  The computer will have
taken over most, if not all, of the tasks.
```

6 Save the document using filename PASS2 and print a copy.

Passage 3

Filename: PASS3
Format the document as follows:

set left margin of 1.5″
set right margin of 1″
single line spacing

?

DO YOU KNOW?
The spacing for the single quotes in the final paragraph?
How to change both margins of one paragraph of an existing document?

```
What is a window?  I do not mean the holes in the wall
with glass in them, I mean the windows which can be
used on a computer.

With windows you can work on several programs at once,
and you can switch between programs with a few
keystrokes or the click of a mouse button.  Windows
are rectangular areas on the screen which can be
reduced or enlarged to requirements.  Within these
windows you can have simple programs running, such as
a clock or calendar or calculator, or they can be full
programs such as word processing, a spreadsheet or a
database.

Several windows can be used at once but the main one
takes priority on the screen and the remainder are
'hidden' behind the main window.  When these are
required, they are brought to the front of the screen
for working on.
```

1 Save the document using filename PASS3 and print a copy.

?

DO YOU KNOW?
What is meant by 'inset'?
How to replace words in existing text?

2 Recall document PASS3.

3 Inset the third paragraph by 1″ on both sides.

4 Change the third paragraph to double line spacing.

5 Replace the words in the following text on windows with those indicated.

6 Save and print.

What is a window? I do not mean the holes in the wall with glass in them, I mean the windows which ~~can be used~~ are available on a computer.

With windows you can work on ~~several~~ a number of programs at once, and you can switch between programs with a few keystrokes or the click of a mouse button. Windows are ~~rectangular~~ split areas on the screen which can be reduced or enlarged to requirements. Within these windows you can have simple programs ~~running~~ operating, such as a clock or calendar or calculator, or they can be ~~full~~ large programs such as word processing, a spreadsheet or a database.

Several windows can be ~~used~~ opened at once but the main one takes priority on the screen and the remainder are 'hidden' behind the main window. When these are ~~required~~ needed, they are brought to the front of the screen for working on.

Passage 4

Filename: PASS4
Format the document as follows:

set left margin of 1″
set right margin of 1″
double line spacing

Bird watching is a very interesting hobby, but it is a hobby only for the patient. To sit for hours on end in a hide or behind a bush without moving or making a noise, demands a great deal of patience. But for the enthusiast the rewards are great. There are so many different birds to look at in this country, and whole areas of the countryside are set aside for the birds to nest in. The type of bird you will see varies with the time of year.

1 Save using filename PASS4 and print a copy.

2 Recall document PASS4.

3 Inset the whole document 0.5″ from both margins. Remember to allow two line spaces after the heading.

4 Add the following passage as the second paragraph.

5 Change the whole document to single line spacing.

?

DO YOU KNOW?

The spacing to leave between the last paragraph and the added paragraph?

TWITCHERS

Are you a 'twitcher'? Do you know what a twitcher is? If not, you are obviously not a bird watcher. A twitcher is a bird watcher who travels around the country looking at birds. When a new sighting of a rare bird has been made, the twitchers appear by the hundreds. They appear to have their own grapevine.

6 Save and print.

7 Recall document PASS4 and make the following corrections:

Bird watching is ~~a very~~ an interesting hobby, but ~~it is a hobby~~ only for the patient. To sit for hours ~~on end~~ in a hide or behind a bush without moving or making a noise, demands a ~~great deal~~ lot of patience. But for the ~~enthusiast~~ enthusiastic the rewards are great. There are so many different birds to look at in this country, and whole areas of the countryside are set aside for the birds to nest and breed in. The type of bird you will see varies ~~with~~ according to the time of the year.

TWITCHERS

Are you a 'twitcher'? Do you know what a twitcher is? If not, you are ~~obviously~~ not a bird watcher. A twitcher is a bird watcher who travels around the country looking for new sightings of ~~at~~ birds. When a sighting of a rare bird has been ~~seen~~ made, the twitchers appear by the hundreds. They appear to have their own grapevine.

8 Save the document and print a copy.

Passage 5

Filename: PASS5
Format the document as follows:

left margin of 1″
right margin of 0.5″
double line spacing

> Keeping a diary is a must for the secretary and her employer. It is essential that they know when, where and with whom appointments have been made. One of the secretary's jobs is to ensure that her employer's diary is kept up-to-date and that appointments are not double booked altogether.
>
> To carry out this job efficiently, the secretary must have the full co-operation of her employer. He must understand that he cannot go ahead and make appointments without informing her that he has done so. If he does, there is bound to be an occasion when two appointments have been made, and two important clients arrive within minutes of each other. This can cause a great deal of embarrassment, not to mention the possible loss of contracts.

1 Save the document using filename PASS5 and print a copy.

2 Recall document PASS5.

3 Add the following as the final paragraph in single line spacing.

4 Inset the final paragraph 1″ from both margins.

?

DO YOU KNOW?
How to add a paragraph in a different line spacing to the rest of the document?
How to add a paragraph with different margins to the rest of the document?

> The good secretary protects her employer from himself. She copes with the day-to-day organisational details and leaves him free to cope with the demands of the business.

5 Save and print.

6 Recall document PASS5 and make the following corrections:

> Keeping a diary is a must for both the secretary and her employer. It is ~~essential~~ necessary that they know when, where and with whom appointments have been made. One of the secretary's ~~jobs~~ tasks is to ensure that her employer's diary is ~~kept~~ up-to-date and that appointments are not double booked. ~~altogether~~.

```
To carry out this job efficiently, the secretary must
have the full co-operation of her employer.  He must
understand that he cannot ~~go ahead and~~ make
                          letting        know
appointments without ~~informing~~ her/that he has done
                 are                           s
so.  If he does, there ~~is~~ bound to be ~~an~~ occasion^ when
two appointments have been made, and two important
clients arrive within minutes of each other.  This ~~can~~
causes                               to all parties
~~cause~~ a great deal of embarrassment/, not to mention
the possible loss of contracts.

               must always
The good secretary/ protects(s) her employer from himself.
 should
She/copes(s) with the day-to-day organisational details
and leaves(s) him free to cope with the ~~demands of the~~
         demands
business/.
```

Passage 6

Filename: PASS6
Format the document as follows:

left margin of 1″
right margin of 1″
double line spacing

```
Did you know that the home is one of the most
dangerous places to be in?  If not, look at the
statistics published on accidents in the home.  Every
year roughly 6,000 people die as a result of accidents
in the home or garden.  This is considerably more than
are killed in accidents in the workplace.

Fire is one of the most common causes of death.
During the past twelve months, how many reports have
you seen on television of children and adults dying in
house fires?  The smoke and fumes are the most common
cause, affecting the individual long before the flames
reach them.
```

1 Save the document using filename PASS6 and print a copy.

2 Recall document PASS6.

3 Change the whole passage to single line spacing.

4 Add the following passage as the third paragraph.

5 Inset the third paragraph 0.5″ from each margin.

```
If this is the case, what can be done about it?  Fit a
smoke alarm in the hallway and on the upstairs
landing.  When smoke is detected, the alarm will ring
and will give sufficient warning for the occupants to
leave the house, call the fire brigade and wait
outside until the fire can be put out.
```

6 Save and print.

7 Recall document PASS6.

8 Change both left and right margins to 1.5″.

9 Change all paragraphs to double line spacing.

10 Make the following changes to the passage:

```
Did you know that your ~~the~~ home is one of the most
dangerous places to be in?  If not, look at the
statistics ~~published~~ on accidents which happen in the home.  Every
year nearly ~~roughly~~ 6,000 people die as a result of accidents
in the home or garden.  This is ~~considerably~~ more than
are killed in accidents in the workplace.

Fire is one of the ~~most~~ common causes of death.
During the past twelve months, how many reports have
you seen on television of both children and adults dying in
house fires?  The smoke and the fumes are the most common
cause - these affect ~~affecting~~ the individual long before the flames
reach them.

If this is so ~~the case~~, what can be done about it? It is wise to fit a
smoke alarm in the hallway and on the upstairs
landing.  When the smoke is detected, an ~~the~~ alarm will ring
giving ~~and will give~~ sufficient warning for the occupants to
leave the house, call out the fire brigade and wait
outside until the fire has been ~~can be~~ put out.
```

Check The spacing between the paragraphs.

11 Save and print.

Passage 7

Filename: PASS7
Format the document as follows:

left margin of 1.5″
right margin of 1″
double line spacing

```
DISK OPERATING SYSTEM

DOS is short for Disk Operating System, and allows the
individual to carry out the housekeeping tasks which
are essential to the smooth running of the system.
One of the facilities available through DOS helps the
organisation of the work on the disk.

The directory of the disk is made up of the names of
the documents as they are created.  The larger the
memory capacity of the disk, the longer and more
unwieldy become the directories.  Using DOS, it is
possible to group the files into smaller directories
and sub-divide the work on the disk so that it can be
found more easily.
```

1 Save the document as filename PASS7 and print a copy.

2 Recall document PASS7.

3 Change the whole passage to single line spacing.

4 Add the following text in single spacing as the first paragraph.

5 Inset the whole passage by 1″ from the left margin.

? DO YOU KNOW?
How to add a paragraph to the beginning of a piece of text?
How to inset the whole passage by 1″ from the left margin?

```
All computers need an operating system of some kind.
Without one, they would simply stare back waiting to
be told what to do.  They are simply pieces of
equipment, and only carry out the instructions put in
by the human in charge.
```

6 Save and print.

7 Recall document PASS7.

8 Change the second paragraph to double spacing.

9 Make the following changes to the passage:

DISK OPERATING SYSTEM

DOS is short for Disk Operating System, and ~~allows~~ [enables] the individual to carry out ~~the~~ [those] housekeeping tasks which are essential to the ~~smooth~~ running of the system. One of the facilities [which is] available through DOS [is to] help~~s~~ the organisation of the work on the disk.

The directory [or catalogue] of the disk is made up of the names of the documents as they are created. The larger the memory capacity of the disk, the ~~longer~~ ~~and~~ more unwieldy become the directories. Using DOS, it is possible to group the files into smaller directories and sub-divide the work on the disk so that it can be found ~~more~~ easily.

All computers ~~need~~ [require] an operating system of some kind. Without one, they would simply stare back [at the operator] waiting to be told what to do. ~~They are simply~~ [The computer is a simple] piece~~s~~ of equipment, an~~d~~ [can] only carry out the instructions put in by the human in charge.

10 Save and print.

TASK 2 *Objectives* 01, 02, 03, 04, 05, 06, 08, 09, 10

1 Create a document called FIRES.

2 Format the document as follows:

left margin of 1″
right ragged margin of 0.5″
single line spacing
block paragraphs

?

DO YOU KNOW?
What is meant by a 'default' setting?
What the default settings are for the program in use?
How many spaces are left between paragraphs in single spacing?
What is meant by a ragged right margin?

How a ragged right margin is achieved on your program?
What a block paragraph is?

3 Key in the following passage:

> OPEN FIRES
>
> An open fire is the centre of attraction in any room. During the winter months what more could you want than to walk into a room and be greeted by the glow of red hot coals burning in the grate? It gives a feeling of security and friendship that is very difficult to find in a radiator. When one thinks of an open fire, the picture conjured up is one of cold, wet weather outside, and inside the fire burning brightly, a brass fender and companion set gleaming by the fireside. But is this the reality?
>
> There is another side to this glowing scene. In the morning when it needs cleaning, dirty ashes need to be taken out and disposed of, the brasses need to be polished and kept in the bright shining state. What picture is conjured up when the fire goes out on a cold day and needs to be relit?

4 Proofread the text carefully – aim for no errors.

5 Save the text and print one copy.

?

DO YOU KNOW?
How to save the text?
How to set up for printing the text?

6 Recall the document and make the following format changes:

right margin to 1.5″
left margin to 1″
double line spacing

?

DO YOU KNOW?
How to change margins within a document?
How to change single spacing to double line spacing?
How many character spaces there are in 1.5″ on your program?
How to make the distinction between block paragraphs in double line spacing?

7 Add the following as the *last* paragraph:

> Before deciding whether or not to install an open fire, weigh up all the pros and cons, and then make a decision based on all the factors, and not on the pictures in the mind.

8 Save the text and print one copy.

9 Recall the document and add the following text as the *third* paragraph. Use the following format for this additional paragraph:

single line spacing
inset 0.5″ from the left margin

DO YOU KNOW?

The spacing required between paragraphs in single and double spacing?

Do you have the time to deal with this type of fire? Do you mind getting your hands dirty? Do you mind coming into a cold house when the fire has gone out?

10 Make the following amendments to the passage:

OPEN FIRES

An open fire ~~is~~ can be the centre of attraction in any room. During the cold winter months what more could you want than to walk into a room and be greeted by ~~the glow of~~ red hot coals burning in the grate? It gives a feeling of comfort, security and friendship that is ~~very~~ difficult to find in a radiator. When one thinks of an open fire, the picture conjured up in the mind is one of cold, wet weather outside, and inside the fire burning brightly, with a brass fender and companion set gleaming by the fireside. ~~But is this the reality?~~ Is this really the case?

There is another side to this glowing scene. It is a fireplace in ~~In~~ the morning when it needs cleaning, and the dirty ashes need to be taken out and disposed of, the brasses must ~~need to~~ be polished to be ~~and~~ kept in the bright shining state. What picture is conjured up when the fire goes out on a cold day and needs to be ~~d~~ relit?

Do you have the time and the patience to deal with this type of fire? Do you mind getting your hands dirty? Do you mind coming into a cold damp house when the fire has gone out?

Before deciding whether ~~or not~~ to install an open fire, weigh up ~~all~~ the pros and cons, and ~~then~~ make a decision based on all the factors, and not on the pictures in the mind.

11 Save and print one copy.

TASK 3 *Objectives* 01, 02, 03, 04, 06, 08, 09, 010, 011

1 Create a document called TILES.

2 Format the document as follows:

left margin of 1″
right ragged margin of 0.5″
double spacing
indented paragraphs

? DO YOU KNOW?

How to set a tab stop?

How many spaces to indent for an indented paragraph?

What spacing to leave between idented paragraphs in double spacing?

Do you know the difference between a dash and a hyphen?

What spacing do you leave on either side of a dash?

3 Key in the following passage:

```
DECORATIVE TILES

    At the beginning of the century, architects used
decorative tiles to cover the inside but also the
outside of buildings.  They were hardwearing and
easily cleaned, and had many different patterns and
designs glazed on to them.  Many subjects were
depicted on these tiles - from fairy tales to simple
leaf patterns.

    Tiles are coming back into fashion, and the sizes
and patterns of tiles available today vary
considerably.  Fruit and vegetable patterns can be put
on to the kitchen walls, plain tiles can be put on to
the walls of the utility room, and there are many
different patterns available for the bathroom walls.
There are even tiles for putting on to the ceilings of
rooms to hide unsightly cracks and uneven surfaces.
```

4 Proofread the copy carefully.

5 Save the document and set the printer to the top of form. Print one copy.

? DO YOU KNOW?

What is meant by a justified right margin?

How to justify the right margin?

How to centre a heading?

6 Recall the document and make the following format changes:

right justified margin of 1.5″
left margin of 1″
single spacing

7 Centre the heading.

8 Add the following text as the *second* paragraph:

> Many public buildings today still show signs of the tiles of the early 20th century, although they do look slightly worse for wear.

Check That the line spacing between the paragraphs is correct.

9 Make the corrections as shown on the text below headed 'Decorative tiles'.

10 Save the document and print the text.

> DECORATIVE TILES ⟶ [centre]
>
> At the beginning of the century, architects used ~~decorative~~ tiles to cover [not only] the inside but also the outside of buildings. They were hardwearing and easily cleaned, and had many ~~different~~ patterns and designs glazed on to them. Many subjects were [shown] ~~depicted~~ on these tiles - from fairy tales [and nursery rhymes] to simple leaf patterns.
>
> Many public buildings ~~today~~ still show signs of the tiles of the early [19th and] 20th century, although they do look slightly worse for wear.
>
> Tiles are [now] ~~coming~~ back [in] ~~into~~ fashion, and the sizes and patterns of tiles available today vary considerably. [There are tiles for all purposes.] Fruit and vegetable patterns can be put on to the kitchen walls, plain tiles [for] ~~can be put on to~~ the walls of the utility room, and there [is a wide] ~~are many~~ [variety of] ~~different~~ patterns available for ~~the~~ bathroom walls. There are even tiles for putting on to the ceilings of rooms to hide [any] unsightly cracks and uneven surfaces.

TASK 4 *Objectives* 01, 02, 03, 05, 010, 011

1 Create a document called GOLF.

2 Format the document as follows:

left margin of 1.5″
right margin of 1″
double spacing
blocked paragraphs

DO YOU KNOW?

What spacing to use before and after single quotes?

3 Key in the following passage:

> WHO GOES FIRST?
>
> A friend of mine has recently taken up golf, and feels very strongly about the etiquette of the game. When watching the golfers on television, he had often wondered what rules governed 'who goes first' off the tee. Is there a special way of determining this or is it a matter of who walks on to the tee first? I decided to try to help him by setting down the general principles involved in deciding the 'honour' as it is called.
>
> If the game is a social one at club level, the general rule is that the player with the lowest handicap tees off first. If, however, two players have equal handicaps, they will 'toss for it' - perhaps by tossing a coin.

4 Proofread the copy carefully and correct any errors.

5 Save the document and print one copy.

6 Recall the document and make the following format changes:

single spacing
justified right margin

DO YOU KNOW?

What spacing to use before and after an apostrophe s?

7 Add the following as a *final* paragraph:

> If the game is being played as part of a competition, whether local or international, there is usually a draw and the players follow the order of the draw. In competitions where there are more than two rounds, the order of play for the third and subsequent rounds is usually determined by the scores. Those with the highest scores go out first, and those with the lowest scores will go out last. If there are equal scores, the competitors will draw for the honour. The theory behind this is that the winner of the tournament will be the last in the clubhouse. That is, if he retains his lead after that day's play.

8 Reformat the last paragraph to double line spacing and justified right margin.

9 Make the following corrections to the passage.

10 Save the document and print one copy.

WHO GOES FIRST?

A friend of mine has recently taken up the game of golf, and feels ~~very~~ strongly about the etiquette of the game. When watching the world famous golfers on television, he had ~~often~~ wondered what the rules were that governed 'who goes first' off the tee. Is there a ~~special~~ definite way of ~~determining~~ deciding this or is it simply a matter of who walks on to the tee first? I decided to try to help him by setting down the ~~general~~ principles involved in deciding the 'honour' as it is called.

If the game is a social one at club level, the ~~general~~ rule is that the player with the lowest handicap tees off first. If, however, there are two players ~~have~~ with equal handicaps, they will 'toss for it' - perhaps by tossing a coin.

If the game is ~~being~~ played as part of a competition, whether at a local or international level, there is ~~usually~~ normally a draw and the players follow the order of the draw. In competitions where there are more than two rounds, the order of play for the third and subsequent rounds is ~~usually~~ determined by the scores. Those with the highest scores will go out first, and those with the lowest scores will go out last. If ~~there are equal scores~~ the scores are equal, the competitors will draw for the honour. The theory behind this is that the winner of the tournament will be the last player in the clubhouse. That is, if he retains his lead after that day's play.

TASK 5 *Objectives* 01, 02, 03, 04, 05, 06, 07, 08, 09, 010, 011

1 Create a document called CARAVANS.

2 Format the document as follows:

left margin of 1″
right justified margin of 1″
single spacing
blocked paragraphs

3 Key in the following passage:

```
CARAVANS AND CARAVANNING

Travelling on any major road during July and August,
it is impossible not to notice the increasing number
of caravans trailing behind cars of all shapes and
sizes.  The caravans range from the very basic to the
luxurious.

When deciding which caravan to buy, it is important
to check that the car which will be used to tow is
capable of pulling that weight.  If not, the engine
of the car and the bodywork and suspension will
suffer.  Never tow if the kerbside weight of the
caravan is in excess of the car manufacturer's stated
towing limit.

The interiors of the caravans vary considerably - the
higher the cost, the more luxurious the interior.
Some of the luxury features available include fitted
carpets, toilet and washroom, single or double beds,
hot water, underfloor heating, to name but a few.

The attraction of the caravan to a family is one of
cost.  Once purchased, it can be used all year and
for any length of time - from an overnight stay 20
miles away to 6 weeks' touring on the Continent.  The
accommodation can be extended by fitting one of the
many awnings which are available at prices starting
from as low as £100.
```

4 Proofread, save the document and print one copy.

5 Recall the document and make the following format changes:

ragged right margin
indented paragraphs

? DO YOU KNOW?
How to delete a paragraph?

6 Delete the paragraph which starts 'The interiors of the caravans . . .'.

7 Insert the following paragraph as a *final* paragraph:

```
The family of today demands all the home comforts
when hiring or buying a caravan, and the
manufacturers are doing their best to meet these
demands.  Depending upon the size of your pocket, the
caravan you purchase could be as well fitted out as
your home.
```

8 Delete the paragraph which starts 'When deciding which . . .'.

9 Make the following corrections to the text:

```
CARAVANS AND CARAVANNING                    June,

Travelling on any major road during July and August,
                              see
it is impossible not to ~~notice~~ the increasing number
                  being pulled
of caravans ~~trailing~~ behind cars of all shapes and

sizes.  The caravans range from the ~~very~~ basic to the

luxurious.

   main
The attraction of the caravan to a family is one of
                                  at any time of
cost.  Once purchased, it can be used ~~all~~ the year
                                              no more than
and for any length of time - from an overnight stay

20 miles away to 6 weeks' touring on the Continent.
T
(t)he accommodation can be extended by fitting one of
                                now
the many awnings which are available at prices
which start
~~starting~~ from as low as £100.

The family of today demands ~~all the~~ home comforts

when hiring or buying a caravan, and the
                             attempting
manufacturers are ~~doing their best~~ to meet these

demands.  Depending upon ~~the size of~~ your pocket, the

caravan you purchase could be as well fitted out as

your home.
```

10 Save the document and print one copy.

TASK 6 *Objectives* 01, 02, 03, 04, 05, 06, 07, 08, 09, 010, 011

1 Create a document called MUSEUMS.

2 Format the document as follows:

decide upon the margins yourself
single spacing
centre the heading

3 Key in the following passage:

```
MUSEUMS!

Museums are dull and boring, and only house dusty
objects which are thousands of years old.  Is this
what the word means to you?  Unfortunately, it is how
many people think of them.  Today, however, this image
is changing.  No longer does an article need to be
thousands of years old to achieve a place in a museum.

The technology of moving pictures has advanced rapidly
during this century, and some of the earlier
techniques and equipment are already lost to future
generations.  Film is destroyed, cameras fall out of
use, and very little thought given to the uniqueness
of some of these artifacts.
```

?

DO YOU KNOW?

How to add more text to an existing paragraph?

4 Add the following to the end of the text immediately after 'these artifacts.'

```
For artifacts are what they are.  They are a record of
part of the history of the twentieth century, and as
we approach the twenty-first century, it is hoped that
some of these will be preserved.
```

5 Proofread, save the document and print one copy.

6 Recall the document and add the following two paragraphs to the end of the document.

```
Fortunately, there is MOMI, the Museum of Moving
Image, which was opened in the South Bank Arts Centre
in London during 1988.  It was built at a cost of some
£10 million, all of which was raised privately.  It is
open to the public every day of the week, except
Mondays, throughout the year.

What is so different about MOMI?  The exhibits in most
museums are behind glass cases and, even if open to
the public touch, there is a definite 'hands off'
policy.  MOMI expects the visitors to take part in the
museum and the exhibits - to touch and use them.  It
is well worth a visit for the moving image buff.
```

?

DO YOU KNOW?

How to change the spacing of part of a document?

How to justify the margins of part of a document?

7 Inset the paragraph which starts 'Fortunately . . .' 1″ from both margins.

8 Change the inset paragraph to double spacing and justified right margin. The remainder of the text is to have a ragged right margin.

9 Delete the paragraph which starts 'Museums are dull . . .'.

10 Save the document and print one copy.

11 Recall Task 6 and delete the paragraph starting 'What is so different . . .'.

12 Make the following changes to the text:

MUSEUMS! Centre

TYPIST: Use unbolted for first para

The technology of ~~moving~~ pictures has advanced very rapidly during this century, and some of the earlier techniques and equipment are already lost to future generations. Film is destroyed, cameras fall out of use, and ~~very~~ little thought is given to the uniqueness of ~~some of~~ these artifacts. For artifacts is what they are. They are a record ~~of part~~ of the history of the 20th ~~twentieth~~ century, and as we approach the 21st ~~twenty first~~ century, it is hoped that some of these will be preserved.

Fortunately, there is MOMI, the Museum of Moving Image, which ~~was~~ opened in the South Bank Arts Centre in London in ~~during~~ 1988. It was built at a cost of ~~some~~ £10 million, all of which was raised by private subscription. ~~privately.~~ It is now open to the general public every day of the week, except Mondays, throughout the year.

13 Save the document and print one copy.

Assignment 1—Word Processing

Section 1 – Objectives 01, 02, 03, 04, 05, 06, 07, 08, 09, *010, *011

Section 2 – Objectives 056, 057, 058, 059, 060, 061, 062, 063, 064, 065, 066, 067

1 Start up the system and load a word processing program.

2 Enter the following text:

```
COLLECTING CIGARETTE CARDS

Collecting cards began almost as soon as the first
cigarette card was issued in 1879, and it is still
going strong with an estimated 50,000 collectors
busily buying and searching for cards.

The earliest known cigarette card is a portrait of
the Marquess of Lorne, and the only copy in existence
is in the Metropolitan Museum of Art in New York.

In England, cards were used as early as 1888 to
strengthen the packets the cigarettes were sold in,
but these were simply advertisements for the
cigarettes they came with.  By the early 1890s,
pictures of actresses were given away with some
brands but it was not until 1894 that the first
proper series of illustrated cards was issued by
Wills with their Three Castles cigarettes.

Before long, the cards were so popular that nearly
all the cigarette makers were forced to put them into
their packets, and from 1900 until 1917 over 1,000
different sets were issued.
```

3 Save the text.

4 Check that the printer is on-line and loaded with paper. Set to top of form and print one copy.

5 Load the document on to the screen and make the following amendments.

6 Delete the paragraph beginning `The earliest known cigarette` ...

7 In the paragraph beginning `In England` ... delete the words `as early as 1888` from the first line.

8 Add the following paragraph as the *next to last* paragraph:

```
These early cards are now the most valuable, and the
most valuable and famous set of all is a pre-1900 card
set of 'Clowns and Circus Artistes'.  When a set of
these came up for auction in 1975, they fetched
£2,000.  The person who sold them had originally
swapped them for two bars of chocolate in 1942!
```

9 In the paragraph beginning `In England` ... add the words `famous actors and` after the phrase `By the early 1890s, pictures of` ...

10 In the first paragraph, replace the words `still going strong` with `very popular`

11 Inset both the left and right margins by five characters and reformat in double spacing with a justified right margin.

12 Save the document and print one copy.

13 Format a blank disk.

14 Copy your assignment on to the blank disk.

15 List the directory of the new disk to prove that the document has been copied accurately.

16 Delete the original file from your workdisk.

17 Close down the system.

Assignment 2—Word Processing

Section 1 – Objectives 01, 02, 03, 04, 05, 06, 07, 08, 09, *010, *011

Section 2 – Objectives 056, 057, 058, 059, 060, 061, 062, 063, 064, 065, 066, 067

1 Start up the system.

2 Format a blank disk.

3 Load a word processing program and enter the following text:

```
EARTHQUAKES IN BRITAIN

On Boxing Day 1979, a strong earthquake shook the
Scottish Border country.  People rushed into the
streets as their furniture moved, doors and windows
rattled and the ornaments danced on tables and
mantlepieces.

Along with the shaking came a rumbling sound like an
express train or heavy lorry passing close by.  Walls
cracked and chimney stacks fell, damaging rooftops in
the cascade of bricks, but miraculously no casualties
were reported.

Britain's greatest earthquakes have generally been
associated with movement along fault lines; in these
cases, after enormous stresses have been built up,
great cracks slice through the earth's crust, moving
rocks very suddenly.

Not all faults are active and, in some cases, time
has healed the rupture and taken away the danger.  In
other instances, the result is the strain of slow
slippage (called 'creep') which does not lead to the
usual sudden catastrophic lurch.
```

4 Save the text.

5 Check that the printer is on-line and the paper is set to top of form. Print one copy.

6 Reload the text on to the screen.

7 In the first paragraph, insert the words `and parts of Northern England` after `Scottish Border country.`

8 Insert the following as the *final* paragraph:

```
In 1988, there were a number of minor earthquakes in
the world, but an earthquake in the Armenian area of
Russia reached disaster proportions with great loss of
life and destruction of property.  When compared with
this we, in Britain, can count ourselves to be very
lucky.
```

9 Delete the words `in the cascade of bricks` in the second paragraph.

10 Delete the paragraph beginning `Britain's greatest earthquakes` ....

11 In the paragraph beginning `Not all faults` replace the words `taken away the danger.` with `helped to solve the problem.`

12 Reformat the document as follows:

(a) inset the final paragraph by five characters on both sides.
(b) the inset paragraph should be in double line spacing and ragged right margin. The remainder of the text should be in single line spacing with a justified right margin.

13 Save the text and print one copy.

14 Make a copy of the saved file on the newly formatted blank disk.

15 Check the directory to ensure that the file has been copied correctly.

16 Delete the file originally saved.

17 Close down the system.

2 Improve your display

Abbreviations

All abbreviations should be typed out in full unless they are on the list of recognised abbreviations. The following are some examples of the recognised abbreviations.

Example NB, etc, eg, ie, & (in Company Name, in Mr & Mrs, and in an address 12 & 13), Dr (Doctor).

Centring

This is carried out automatically by most word processing programs and the facility should be used to ensure accuracy.

A piece of text which has been centred is positioned *exactly* in the middle of the space between the left and the right margins.

Example

```
LM                             C                             RM
10                             40                            70

                      WORD PROCESSING

                      32            46
```

In a word with an odd number of characters, the odd character will be placed consistently either to the left or to the right of centre.

Embolden

To embolden means to emphasise specific words or lines. The emboldening may not show on the screen, as it is a command to the printer, and will show on the final printout in one of two ways:

- the letter is printed once, and then a second time directly on top of the first;
- the letter is printed once, and then a second time fractionally to the right – known as 'shadow printing'.

Embolden is an alternative term for 'bold'.

Margins

TOP/BOTTOM

These two margins are usually determined when the word processing package is installed. Sometimes they can be changed within the document if necessary.

LEFT/RIGHT

The left and right margins of text are either predetermined on installation, or if they are likely to change with every document, they can be set as desired.

The normal margins are 1″ on the left and 0.5″ on the right. They can be changed usually by 0.5″ on either one side or on both sides. If this is done, it can aid display.

There are two types of right margin:

Justified right margin With a justified right margin, the text stops at exactly the same place on the line and gives the document a box-like appearance. This is achieved either by spaces being added between the words, or by adjusting the characters on the line giving equal spaces on either side of words.

Ragged right margin A ragged right margin is of irregular appearance with equal spaces between words.

INSET PARAGRAPHS/PASSAGE

To inset a *paragraph* is to widen the margins of that paragraph only, so that it stands out. One or both margins can be changed.

Example original margins positions 10 and 75
inset 0.5″ on both margins
new margins (for that paragraph only) positions 15 and 70

To inset a *passage* is to widen the margins of the whole passage. This does not make it stand out, but it can be used to improve the display of a passage. This process is also known as *indenting* a paragraph, but would normally refer to the left margin only. Indenting can also mean starting a paragraph ½″ in on the first line.

Example The following example shows all of the above points:

```
Margins 10 and 75 - Ragged Right Margin

This is a sample paragraph to show the effects of margins within
a document.  The effect changes according to the margins used and
can be used to alter the appearance of a document, and to make
full use of the page length.

Left margin indented 5 spaces - right margin as before

     This is a sample paragraph to show the effects of margins
     within a document.  The effect changes according to the
     margins used and can be used to alter the appearance of a
     document, and to make full use of the page length.

Both left and right margins inset by 5 spaces

     This is a sample paragraph to show the effects of
     margins within a document.  The effect changes
     according to the margins used and can be used to alter
     the appearance of a document, and to make full use of
     the page length.

Margins 10 and 75 - justified right margin

This is a sample paragraph to show the effects of margins within
a document.  The effect changes according to the margins used and
can be used to alter the appearance of a document, and to make
full use of the page length.

Left margin indented 5 spaces - JUSTIFIED right margin as before

     This is a sample paragraph to show the effects of margins
     within a document.  The effect changes according to the
     margins used and can be used to alter the appearance of a
     document, and to make full use of the page length.

Both left and right margins inset by 5 spaces - justified right
margin

     This is a sample paragraph to show the effects of
     margins within a document.  The effect changes
     according to the margins used and can be used to alter
     the appearance of a document, and to make full use of
     the page length.
```

Check Note how much easier it is to see the effects of the display with a justified margin.

Open punctuation

It is common practice today to omit all unnecessary punctuation. This does not include the punctuation required for grammatical purposes.

In open punctuation, there are no full stops within:

- a name and address on a letter
- a date eg 12 November 1989 1 May 1976 30 June 1991
- a reference
- abbreviations eg Mr Mrs NB etc MP BSc

Paragraphs

There are three basic types of paragraph as shown below:

BLOCK PARAGRAPHS

All lines start at the left margin.

Example

```
This is a sample of a block paragraph.  All
the lines start at the left margin, and it
is very easy to display.

The second paragraph would therefore look
like this.  Note how easy it is to see the
distinction between the paragraphs.
```

INDENTED PARAGRAPHS

The first line of *every* paragraph starts half-an-inch from the left margin.

Example

```
     This is a sample of an indented
paragraph.

     Note how the first line starts half an
inch from the left margin (either 5 or 6
spaces depending upon the type size being
used) and all other lines start at the left
margin.
```

HANGING PARAGRAPHS

The first line starts at the left margin, and second and subsequent lines start consistently two or three spaces in from the left margin.

Example

```
This is a sample of a hanging paragraph.  In
   this type of paragraph, the first line
   starts at the left margin.

All other lines start consistently 2 or 3
   spaces in from the margin.
```

Spacing

ALLOCATING SPACE

Horizontally One inch can include as many characters as the printer can cope with, but the usual numbers are 10 or 12.

Vertically One inch is equal to six *clear* line spaces.

LINE SPACING – BLOCK PARAGRAPHS

Single spacing No blank lines within the paragraph, but there must be *one* clear line space between paragraphs.

```
This short paragraph shows the effect of
leaving an extra line space between blocked
paragraphs in single line spacing.

If a clear line space is not left, the
distinction between the paragraphs is not
clear.
```

Double spacing One line space between each line within the paragraph, but there must be at least *two* clear spaces between the paragraphs.

```
This short paragraph shows the effect of

leaving an extra line space between blocked

paragraphs in double line spacing.


If an extra clear line space is not left, the

distinction between the paragraphs is not

obvious.
```

LINE SPACING – INDENTED PARAGRAPHS

When text is typed using indented paragraphs, there need only be *one* clear line space, whether in double or single spacing. This is because the indent gives the distinction between the paragraphs.

Single spacing No blank lines within the paragraph, but there must be *one* clear line space between paragraphs.

```
     This is a sample of text in single line
spacing with indented paragraphs.  The para-
graphs start 5 or 6 spaces in from the left
margin.

     The second paragraph starts at the same
point a clear line space from the first
paragraph.
```

Double spacing One line space between each line within the paragraph, and only *one* clear line space between paragraphs.

Remember Use the facility provided by your program for double line spacing. *Do not put a return at the end of every line.*

```
     This is a short paragraph to show that

there is no need for more than one return at

the end of an indented paragraph when using

double spacing.  One return will be a double

line space.

     The paragraph indent is sufficient to

make the distinction between the paragraphs.
```

SPACING AFTER PUNCTUATION

Use the following guidelines for spacing after punctuation:

One space after	comma (,) semicolon (;)
Two spaces after	full stop (.) question mark (?) exclamation mark (!) colon (:)
One space before and one space after	dash (–)
One space before and no space after	opening double quotes (“) opening brackets (
No space before and one space after	closing double quotes (”) closing brackets)
No space before and no space after	hyphen (-) apostrophe (’) before “s”

Type sizes

The most common type sizes are 10 characters to the inch and 12 characters to the inch. Some printers allow the size of the type face to be changed within a document. The following is an example of some of these changes of type sizes. They can be used to good effect when diplaying a document.

This is an example of 5 characters per inch.

This is an example of 10 characters per inch.

This is an example of 17 characters per inch.

This is an example of 20 characters per inch.

3 Spreadsheet

?

DO YOU KNOW?

What a *column* is?

What a *row* is?

What a *cell* is?

How to move about the spreadsheet?

How to move to a specified cell?

What to do if an error is made during keying-in?

How to save a spreadsheet?

TASK 1 **Filename: SS1**

1 Key in the spreadsheet *exactly* as shown. If necessary, use the step-by-step instructions following the spreadsheet.

2 Start in cell A1.

ANNUAL VIDEO HIRE				
TYPE	1st Qtr	2nd Qtr	3rd Qtr	4th Qtr
Comedy	235	175	221	256
Horror	321	246	319	97
SciFi	192	382	377	185
Thriller	310	199	401	221

?

DO YOU KNOW?

What a 'trailing zero' is?

3 When keying in the spreadsheet, do not worry if the figures show 'trailing zeros', ie 235.00. These will be dealt with later.

4 The following are step-by-step instructions on the keying in of the above spreadsheet. If you have any doubt about keying in, follow these instructions carefully:

(a) Position the cursor in cell A1.
(b) Type: ANNUAL VIDEO HIRE in capital letters. *Note*: It should go across into cell B1.
(c) Move the cursor to cell A2.
(d) Type: TYPE in capital letters.
(e) Complete the spreadsheet as follows:

B2	1st Qtr	A5	SciFi
C2	2nd Qtr	B5	192
D2	3rd Qtr	C5	382
E2	4th Qtr	D5	377
A3	Comedy	E5	185
B3	235	A6	Thriller
C3	175	B6	310
D3	221	C6	199
E3	256	D6	401
A4	Horror	E6	221
B4	321		
C4	246		
D4	319		
E4	97		

(f) When completed, the spreadsheet should look like this:

	A	B	C	D	E
1	ANNUAL VIDEO HIRE				
2	TYPE	1st Qtr	2nd Qtr	3rd Qtr	4th Qtr
3	Comedy	235	175	221	256
4	Horror	321	246	319	97
5	SciFi	192	382	377	185
6	Thriller	310	199	401	221

(g) Save the spreadsheet, using filename SS1.

Do not delete any of the spreadsheets until you are told to do so. They are recalled and used again.

?

DO YOU KNOW?

How to print a spreadsheet?

How to set the printer to 'top of form'?

TASK 2 Filename: SS2

1 Enter the following spreadsheet using every line and every space as shown in Task 1 of this section.

2 Start in cell A1.

BOWLING FIGURES				
BOWLER	OVERS	MAIDENS	RUNS	WICKETS
Andrews	31	6	100	2
Bradley	27	5	110	1
Owens	26	2	49	2
Smith	20	0	81	3

3 Save the document using filename SS2 and print one copy.

?

DO YOU KNOW?

How to recall a spreadsheet?

How to insert a blank row?

TASK 3 **1** Recall spreadsheet SS1.

2 Print one copy.

3 Insert a blank row between:

`Annual Video Hire` and `Type`

`Type` and `Comedy`

4 Save the spreadsheet using filename SS1 and print a copy. If you cannot print out as and when you wish, change the filename to SS1a, SS1b etc and print a copy at a later time.

TASK 4

1 Recall spreadsheet SS2.

2 Insert a blank row between:

`Bowling Figures` and `Bowler`

`Bowler` and `Andrews`

3 Save the spreadsheet using filename SS2 and print a copy.

4 *Compare* the two printouts for each spreadsheet. See how clearly the data stands out from the headings with the blank rows between them.

TASK 5

In Tasks 3 and 4, blank rows were inserted to help the display. In this and the next task, blank rows are inserted to enable data to be added.

1 Recall spreadsheet SS1.

2 Insert a blank row between `SciFi` and `Thriller` .

3 Insert the following data into that blank row:

Sport	26	79	110	125

4 Type the word TOTAL in cell A11 and leave the remainder of the row blank.

5 Save the spreadsheet and print a copy.

6 The spreadsheet should now look like this:

	A	B	C	D	E
1	ANNUAL VIDEO HIRE				
2					
3	TYPE	1st Qtr	2nd Qtr	3rd Qtr	4th Qtr
4					
5	Comedy	235	175	221	256
6	Horror	321	246	319	97
7	SciFi	192	382	377	185
8	Sport	26	79	110	125
9	Thriller	310	199	401	221
10					
11	TOTAL				

TASK 6

1 Recall spreadsheet SS2.

2 The bowling figures for Jones need to be added, but remember to keep the names in alphabetical order.

Jones	25	3	64	1

3 Type the word TOTAL in cell A11.

4 Save the spreadsheet and print a copy.

?

DO YOU KNOW?
How to insert a blank column?

TASK 7

1 Recall spreadsheet SS1.

2 Insert an extra column between `2nd Qtr` and `3rd Qtr` .

3 Insert an extra row between `TYPE` and `COMEDY` .

4 Insert a heading in the blank column, using two rows and typing in – `HALF YR` and `TOTAL`

5 Insert a heading in column G, using two rows and typing in – `FULL YR` and `TOTAL`

6 Save the spreadsheet and print a copy.

7 The spreadsheet should now look like this:

	A	B	C	D	E	F	G
1	ANNUAL VIDEO HIRE						
2							
3	TYPE	1st Qtr	2nd Qtr	HALF YR	3rd Qtr	4th Qtr	FULL YR
4				TOTAL			TOTAL
5							
6	Comedy	235	175		221	256	
7	Horror	321	246		319	97	
8	SciFi	192	382		377	185	
9	Sport	26	79		110	125	
10	Thriller	310	199		401	221	
11							
12	TOTAL						

TASK 8

1 Recall spreadsheet SS2.

2 Insert an extra column between `RUNS` and `WICKETS` with the heading on two rows as follows: `AV RUNS`
`PER OVER`

Remember to insert a blank row between the headings and the data.

3 Save the spreadsheet and print a copy.

?

DO YOU KNOW?
What a *formula* is?
What putting in a formula in a cell does?
The formula for adding rows and columns together?
The symbol for *addition*?

TASK 9

1 Set up a spreadsheet as described in Task 1, using the filename FORMULA.

2 Key in the following figures in cells A1, A2, A3 and A4 respectively:

250	325	345	564

3 Key in the following figures in cells B1, B2, B3 and B4 respectively:

12	24	54	67

4 In cell A6, put the formula for adding all the figures in column A.

What is it? ______________________________

Note how quickly the TOTAL was calculated. The *answer* will also be *accurate*. This indicates the two major reasons for using a formula – *speed* and *accuracy*.

5 In cell B6, put the formula for adding all the figures in column B.

What is it? ______________________________

6 In cell C1, put the formula for adding cells A1 and B1 together.

What is it? ______________________________

7 Add cells A2 and B2 together — put the formula in cell C2.

8 Add cells A3 and B3 together — put the formula in cell C3.

9 Add cells A4 and B4 together — put the formula in cell C4.

10 Add cells A6 and B6 together — put the formula in cell C6.

11 The spreadsheet should now look like this:

	A	B	C
1	250	12	262
2	325	24	349
3	345	54	399
4	564	67	631
5			
6	1484	157	1641

?

DO YOU KNOW?

The formula for subtracting one cell from another?

The symbol for *subtraction*?

TASK 10

1 In spreadsheet FORMULA, in cell D1 put the formula for subtracting B1 from A1.

What is it? ______________________________

2 Subtract B2 from A2 – put the formula in cell D2.

3 Subtract B3 from A3 – put the formula in cell D3.

4 Subtract B4 from A4 – put the formula in cell D4.

5 Subtract B6 from A6 – put the formula in cell D6.

?

DO YOU KNOW?
The formula for multiplying two cells together?
The symbol for *multiplication*?

TASK 11

1 In spreadsheet FORMULA, in cell E1 put the formula for multiplying A1 by B1.

What is it? ______________________

2 Multiply A2 by B2 – put the formula in cell E2.

3 Multiply A3 by B3 – put the formula in cell E3.

4 Multiply A4 by B4 – put the formula in cell E4.

5 Multiply A6 by B6 – put the formula in cell E6.

?

DO YOU KNOW?
The formula for dividing one cell by another?
The symbol for *division*?

TASK 12

1 In spreadsheet FORMULA, in cell F1 put the formula for dividing A1 by B1.

What is it? ______________________

2 Divide A2 by B2 – put the formula in cell F2.

3 Divide A3 by B3 – put the formula in cell F3.

4 Divide A4 by B4 – put the formula in cell F4.

5 Divide A6 by B6 – put the formula in cell F6.

6 The spreadsheet should now look like this:

	A	B	C	D	E	F
1	250	12	262	238	3000	21
2	325	24	349	301	7800	14
3	345	54	399	291	18630	6
4	564	67	631	497	37788	8
5						
6	1484	157	1641	1327	232988	9

?

DO YOU KNOW?
How to print the spreadsheet?
How to print the contents of the spreadsheet so that the formulae are printed?

TASK 13

1 Print the spreadsheet – it should look like the spreadsheet in Task 12.

2 Print the spreadsheet showing the formulae.

?

DO YOU KNOW?
How to change the contents of a cell?

TASK 14

1 Change the contents of cell B1 from 12 to 24.

2 Print a copy of the amended spreadsheet and circle the differences between the two – the result of the one change in cell B1.

3 The spreadsheet should now look like this.

	A	B	C	D	E	F
1	250	24	274	226	6000	10
2	325	24	349	301	7800	14
3	345	54	399	291	18630	6
4	564	67	631	497	37788	8
5						
6	1484	169	1653	1315	250796	9

Note: The third reason for using a formula – *easy changes to data*. One change has affected *eight* other cells and all of these changes were made *automatically*.

DO YOU KNOW?

How to widen the columns?

How to format to two decimal places for money columns?

What 'replicate' means?

How to replicate/copy formulae on your program?

What is meant by 'condensed' print on a spreadsheet?

How to print a spreadsheet using condensed print?

Note: Money columns should be formatted to two decimal places, otherwise the 'trailing zeros' will be dropped, ie 22.70 will show as 22.7.

TASK 15

1 Change the width of each column to 12.

2 Format all columns for two decimal places.

3 Key in the following figures starting in cell A1:

67.25	1762.29	11725.87
23.63	1498.75	22256.13
45.21	3122.11	34321.98
79.85	8917.15	22161.50

Note: The 'trailing zero' should have printed in C4. If it has not, *check your format*.

4 Use a formula in cell A6 to add column A.

5 Replicate the formula to add columns B and C.

6 Use a formula in cell D1 to add row 1.

7 Replicate that formula to add rows 2, 3 and 4.

8 Save the spreadsheet using filename FORMULA and print a copy.

DO YOU KNOW?

What an 'integer' is?

How to change to integer format?

TASK 16

1 Recall FORMULA and change to integer format for all columns.

2 Use a formula in cell E1 to subtract cell B1 from cell C1.

3 Replicate that formula to subtract cell B2 from C2, cell B3 from C3, cell B4 from C4 and cell B6 from C6.

4 Print the spreadsheet twice – one of the printouts should show the formulae.

5 Use a formula in cell F1 to multiply cell A1 by cell B1.

6 Replicate that formula to multiply cell A2 by B2, cell A3 by B3, cell A4 by B4 and cell A6 by B6.

7 Save the spreadsheet using filename FORMULA and print a copy. (If you have not been able to print FORMULA, use the filename FORMULA1.)

Note: How the figures have been rounded up or down.

?

DO YOU KNOW?

The formula to use when dividing one cell by a figure?

TASK 17

1 It is possible to divide one cell by another cell, or to divide one cell by a figure. In this task you are going to divide cells by different figures.

2 Recall FORMULA (or FORMULA1) and change the format to two decimal places.

3 Use a formula in cell G1 to divide cell C1 by 25.

4 Use a formula in cell G2 to divide cell C2 by 35.

5 Use a formula in cell G3 to divide cell C3 by 15.

6 Use a formula in cell G4 to divide cell C4 by 18.

7 Print two copies of the spreadsheet, showing the formulae in one of them.

8 The spreadsheet will now look like this:

	A	B	C	D	E	F	G
1	67.25	1762.29	11725.87	13555.58	9963.58	118514.00	469.03
2	23.63	1498.75	22256.13	23792.15	20757.38	55858.41	635.89
3	45.21	3122.11	34321.98	37489.30	31199.87	141150.59	2288.13
4	79.85	8917.15	22161.50	31158.50	13244.35	712034.43	1231.19
5							
6	215.94	15300.30	90465.48		75165.18	3303946.78	

TASK 18

1 Recall spreadsheet SS1 if you still have it stored on disk. If not, use your printout to re-key the spreadsheet.

2 Using your knowledge of formulae for adding columns and rows, complete the blank rows and columns. *Remember to replicate formulae wherever possible.*

For HALF YR TOTAL, add columns B and C.
For FULL YR TOTAL, add columns D, E and F.

3 Save the spreadsheet and print two copies – one must show the formulae.

TASK 19

1 Recall spreadsheet SS2 (or retype if necessary using your printout).

2 Find the average runs per over for Andrews by dividing the runs by the overs. Replicate the formula for all bowlers.

3 Format the column to two decimal places.

?

DO YOU KNOW?

How to replicate some, but not all, of the columns?

4 Use a formula to add the number of overs and place on the TOTAL row.

5 Replicate the formula for all columns with the exception of that showing average runs per over.

6 Save the spreadsheet and print two copies – one must show the formulae.

?

DO YOU KNOW?

The default width of each column?

How to change the column width?

How many spaces to leave between columns?

TASK 20

1 Recall spreadsheet SS2.

2 Notice how the headings do not look as though they are attached to the rest of the column.

3 Check each column width – count the longest line and add two for a space.

4 If necessary, change the width of the column.

5 The columns may still look out of alignment.

?

DO YOU KNOW?

What it means to 'right align' a column?

How to right align text for a row?

How to right align text for a column?

6 Right align the text in the headings of all columns but the first.

7 Save the spreadsheet and print a copy.

8 The spreadsheet should now look like this. See the difference – which looks better?

BOWLING FIGURES

BOWLERS	OVERS	MAIDENS	RUNS	AV RUNS PER OVER	WICKETS
Andrews	31	6	100	3.23	2
Bradley	27	5	110	4.07	1
Jones	25	3	64	2.56	1
Owens	26	2	49	1.88	2
Smith	20	0	81	4.05	3
TOTAL	129	16	404		9

?

DO YOU KNOW?

How to delete a row?

How to delete a column?

How to delete a block of cells?

TASK 21

1 Recall SS1.

2 Delete the row for Horror movies.

3 Delete the column for HALF YR TOTAL.

4 The FULL YR TOTAL formulae are now incorrect. Delete the block of cells G6 to G10.

5 Insert the correct formula and replicate.

6 Save the spreadsheet and print a copy.

TASK 22 Delete all the spreadsheets which you have on your workdisk.

TASK 23 *Objectives* 012, 013, 014, 015, 016, 017, 018, *019, *020

1 Set up a spreadsheet for the number of payments required for Framework Metal Detectors.

2 Use the title FRAMEWORK METAL DETECTORS, starting in the first column.

3 Input the following column headings which should be right justified:

NAME	DISCOUNT	NUMBER OF PAYMENTS		
	PRICE	6	12	18

4 In the first column enter the following titles which should be left justified:

```
F1210X
F1225X
F1260X
F1235X
F1265X
F1280X
```

5 Enter the following values into the DISCOUNT PRICE column:

```
169.50
279.50
349.50
362.50
449.50
499.50
```

6 The metal detectors are available on interest-free credit repayable over 6, 12 or 18 months.

7 In the column headed 6 months use a formula to calculate the monthly repayments for the F1210X. Show the figures to two decimal places.

8 Replicate the formula for the remainder of the column.

9 Repeat (7) and (8) for columns headed 12 months and 18 months.

10 Save the spreadsheet and print two copies. One of the printouts should show the formulae which have been used.

11 Recall the spreadsheet.

12 The price of the F1260X has been reduced to £329.50. Make the necessary amendment.

13 Add a final column headed NO SOLD, and add the following figures:

12	10	7	6	1	2

14 In the NAME column add a final row headed TOTAL.

15 In the NO SOLD column only, use a formula to find the total number of metal detectors sold.

16 Save the spreadsheet and print two copies. One of the printouts should show the formulae which have been used.

TASK 24 *Objectives* 012, 013, 014, 015, 016, 017, 018, *019, *020

1 Set up a spreadsheet with a main heading CARAVAN AWNINGS.

2 Input the following column headings:

MODEL	10 FT	11 FT	12 FT	13 FT	14 FT	15 FT

3 In the first column enter the following headings:

Panther
Lion
Tiger
Leopard

4 Enter the following data:

MODEL	10 FT	11 FT
Panther	147	151
Lion	152	157
Tiger	155	161
Leopard	161	168

5 Use a formula to generate the prices of each of the different types of awnings. Replicate formulae where appropriate.

The Panther awnings increase by £4 for each increase of 1 ft.

The Lion awnings increase by £5 for each increase of 1 ft.

The Tiger awnings increase by £6 for each increase of 1 ft.

The Leopard awnings increase by £7 for each increase of 1 ft.

6 Save the spreadsheet and print two copies. One of the copies must show the formulae which have been used.

Assignment 1—Spreadsheet

Section 1 – Objectives 012, 013, 014, 015, 016, 017, 018, *019, *020

Section 2 – Objectives 056, 057, 059, 060, 061, 062, 063, 067, 070

You are going to create a spreadsheet which shows the bargains on offer from a firm of caravan suppliers.

1 Start up the system. Load a spreadsheet program and enter your name and today's date at the top.

2 Enter the following headings across the top of the sheet, starting in the first column:

NAME	SLEEPS	RETAIL	OUR PRICE	SAVINGS

3 Enter the following names in the first column, starting in the row below the headings:

```
Tristar
Alexander
Princess
Romeo
Juliet
```

4 Enter the following figures for the columns SLEEPS, RETAIL, OUR PRICE:

SLEEPS	RETAIL	OUR PRICE
4	7925.76	7617.99
3	8523.23	7355.19
5	7761.60	7355.19
3	7085.75	6622.50
4	8010.20	7500.50

5 Save the spreadsheet.

6 Check that the printer is on-line, the paper is in the printer and set to top of form. Print one copy.

7 Using a formula, calculate the savings for Tristar by subtracting OUR PRICE from the RETAIL. Replicate the formula for the other caravans.

8 Add a column headed NO SOLD and enter the following figures:

4	6	4	5	2

9 Add a final column headed TOTAL SALES.

10 The Alexander caravans have all been sold. Delete the row from the spreadsheet.

11 Calculate the total sales of Tristar by multiplying OUR PRICE by the NO SOLD. Replicate the formula for the other caravans.

12 Add a row between Romeo and Juliet and enter the following figures:

Rayon	2	6920	6500.99	5

13 Add a final row for the TOTALS.

14 Use a formula to calculate the number of caravans sold and the total sales.

15 Print the spreadsheet twice, ensuring that one copy shows the formulae used.

16 Change to integer format.

17 Save the spreadsheet and print a copy.

18 Make a back-up copy of the disk.

19 Delete the original file.

20 Close down the system.

Assignment 2—Spreadsheet

Section 1 – Objectives 012, 013, 014, 015, 016, 017, 018, *019, *020.

Section 2 – Objectives 056, 057, 059, 060, 061, 062, 063, 067, 070, 071

You are going to create a spreadsheet which shows the sales records of car salesmen.

1 Start up the system.

2 Format a blank disk *or* open up an empty user area on a current disk.

3 Load a spreadsheet program and enter your name and today's date at the top.

4 Enter the following headings:

```
SALESMAN    MODEL    COST    NO SOLD
```

5 Enter the following names in the first column, starting in the row below the headings:

```
Peter Taylor
Alan Cross
Mark Brown
David Allen
Clive Rushden
```

6 Enter the following data for the columns headed MODEL, COST and NO SOLD:

MODEL	COST	NO SOLD
T1000	7251.99	4
L750	6176.75	2
M2000	8999.50	3
M2200	8999.99	4
L1500	7500.45	3

7 Save the spreadsheet and print one copy.

8 Add a new column TOTAL SALES. Generate a formula to find the TOTAL SALES of the T1000. Multiply cost by number sold. Replicate the formula for the other models.

9 Add a final column COMMISSION. Generate a formula to find the commission for Peter Taylor. The commission is earned at 10% of the TOTAL SALES. Replicate the formula for the other salesmen.

10 Add a new row between Peter Taylor and Alan Cross as follows:

```
Gerald Masson    T1500    8500.99    2
```

11 The price of the L1500 has been reduced to £7250.00. Make the necessary change.

12 Change the spreadsheet to integer format.

13 Mark Brown has now left the company. Delete his sales record.

14 Add a final row – TOTALS. Use a formula to generate the totals of the NO SOLD, TOTAL SALES and COMMISSION columns.

15 Save the spreadsheet and print two copies showing:

(a) the formulae
(b) the figures showing the expenditure in integer format.

16 Make a back-up copy of the data file.

17 Using the equipment available to you, and following the instructions given to you by your tutor, connect your computer to another source and send the following message:

Name:

I have now completed my CLAIT Spreadsheet assignment.

Date:

18 Close down the system.

4 Databases

TASK 1 *Section 1 – Objectives* 021, 022, 023, 024, 025, 026, 027, *028, *029

?

DO YOU KNOW?
How to load a Database program?
What is meant by a *field*?
What is meant by a *record*?
What is meant by a *file*?
What is meant by a *string*?
What is meant by *numeric*?
What is meant by *alphanumeric*?
How to set up a database?

1. Load the database program.
2. Set up a database using the filename CRUISERS. A FIELD DEFINITION SHEET helps to set up the database accurately. A copy is available in the Teacher's Manual – ask your tutor for a copy.
3. Use the field headings as shown on Data Sheet 1.
4. Enter the data in the 17 records shown on Data Sheet 1.

?

DO YOU KNOW?
How to save the records?
How to set the printer to top of form?
How to print the complete file?

5. Save the file.
6. Print a copy of the complete file.
7. Proofread the data from the printed copy.

?

DO YOU KNOW?
How to amend a field within a record?

8. Amend any errors *before* continuing with the remainder of this Task.

Remember: the maximum number of data entry errors allowed is three – aim for none.

DATA SHEET 1 – DATABASES

CLASS	OVERALL LENGTH	BEAM	NO OF BERTHS	TOP SPEED	ENGINE	PRICE	NAME	NO OF CABINS
A	5.95	2.32	2	40	211	15600	Corgi 465	1
C	8.18	2.85	4	19.5	124	29338	Bull Dog 392	2
D	11.63	4.09	4	21	350	89561	Terrier 2876	2
A	6.50	2.49	2	45	167	16259	Corgi 475	1
B	10.36	3.71	6	35	400	54215	Cheetah 727	2
A	7.75	3	4	34.5	275	33500	Corgi 565	2
B	10.97	3.51	6	23	370	85217	Cheetah 827	2
D	5.95	3.17	6	20	400	92165	Terrier 3876	2
C	8.18	2.95	4	29	370	62316	Bull Dog 1100	2
D	11.63	3.25	7	40	297	262000	Terrier 416	4
A	6.50	3.15	4	25	400	86211	Corgi 921	2
D	17.25	5.41	6	24	1100	259000	Terrier 4876	3
C	11.28	4.11	6	23	450	108000	Bull Dog 1200	3
B	7.01	2.29	3	20	146	15478	Cheetah 612	1
A	9.91	3.23	2	20	260	42000	Corgi 1021	1
D	9.00	2.85	4	40	410	34574	Terrier 5876	2
C	8.23	2.90	4	31	275	29892	Bull Dog 1300	2
NEW RECORDS - GROUP A								
B	10.36	2.95	3	21	200	56000	Cheetah 712	2
A	17.25	3.71	2	45	165	18271	Corgi 1121	1
C	11.28	5.41	6	24	1100	221000	Bull Dog 1400	3
NEW RECORDS - GROUP B								
B	7.01	2.30	3	20	150	17215	Cheetah	1
D	9.91	3.23	2	20	260	43000	Terrier 6876	1
A	9.00	2.85	4	40	410	44574	Corgi 1221	2

?

DO YOU KNOW?

What is meant by *sort*?

What is meant by a *keyfield*?

How to sort by a keyfield?

How to add a record?

How to delete a record?

How to amend a record?

9 Sort the file into *ascending* order of *price*.

10 Add the three new records which are shown on Data Sheet 1 (Group A).

11 Delete the following two records:

```
Cheetah 827
Terrier 416
```

12 The price of the Terrier 2876 should be £79561; make the necessary change.

13 Some modifications have been made and the top speed of the Corgi 921 should now read 30.

14 Save the Database and print one copy.

Keep the database on disk – it is required for later tasks.

TASK 2 *Section 1 – Objectives* 021, 022, 023, 024, 025, 026, 027, *028, *029

1 Load the database program.

2 Set up a file to contain details of the employees who have left your firm. The details are found on Data Sheet 2. Use the field headings as shown on Data Sheet 2 – you can abbreviate them if you wish. The filename is LEAVERS.

Note: It is quicker and easier to proofread as the fields are keyed in – before *the return key is pressed and the fields are entered into the record.*

?

DO YOU KNOW?

What a *code letter* is?

Why code letters are used in a Database file?

3 Use the following Code Letters:

In the REASON FOR LEAVING field:

IH = Ill Health
ER = Early Retirement
ML = Maternity Leave
AA = Another Appointment

In the DEPARTMENT field:

A = Administration
M = Marketing
P = Personnel
S = Sales

4 Save the complete file.

5 Set the printer to top of form and print the complete file.

6 Proofread the copy and make any amendments *before* proceeding with the remainder of the Task.

7 Sort the file into LENGTH OF SERVICE order, the most recent at the beginning.

8 Make the following changes:

```
Joanne Coleman was described as a Typist, when in fact she
is an Audio Typist.  Make the necessary correction.

Donald Harvey was a Clerk in the Marketing Department, not
in the Administration Department as stated.  Make the
correction.

Edward Forest started in the Marketing Department on 4th
May 1977 and had thus had 11 years' service.  Make the two
corrections.
```

9 Add the new records shown on Data Sheet 2 under NEW RECORDS — GROUP A.

10 Delete the records for Mark Philipson and Eric Forshaw.

11 Save the file and print a copy of all records.

Do not delete the file from the disk – it will be needed in later tasks.

DATA SHEET 2 – DATABASES

NAME/REASON FOR LEAVING	DEPARTMENT	DATE OF JOINING	DATE OF LEAVING	LENGTH OF SERVICE	POSITION
ILL HEALTH					
Alex Taylor	Sales	10.11.71	17.1.87	15	Salesman
Andrew Gayner	Marketing	7.7.86	8.9.87	1	Purchase Clerk
Donald Harvey	Admin	4.6.85	7.7.89	4	Clerk
Hilary Cross	Marketing	14.10.81	21.11.83	2	Personal Assistant
Alan Forest	Sales	2.2.81	14.3.89	8	Salesman
Edward Forest	Marketing	4.5.79	3.2.89	9	Marketing Manager
EARLY RETIREMENT					
Graham Shawcross	Sales	15.12.70	29.12.88	18	Salesman
John Dunstan	Personnel	20.5.70	14.6.89	19	Clerk
Michael Taylor	Salesman	15.7.84	23.8.89	5	Salesman
Brian Stanton	Admin	16.12.64	29.12.89	25	Clerical Assistant
MATERNITY LEAVE					
Joanne Coleman	Sales	31.1.80	29.2.86	6	Typist
Annette Johnson	Sales	21.9.80	27.8.82	1	Shorthand Typist
ANOTHER APPOINTMENT					
Philip Casson	Personnel	14.6.82	26.2.89	6	Clerk
Mark Philipson	Personnel	4.2.80	10.2.89	9	Clerk
Eric Forshaw	Personnel	18.8.83	27.9.87	4	Wages Clerk
Dennis Dunstan	Personnel	13.12.75	18.12.88	13	Personnel Officer
Anthony Steele	Sales	15.7.84	23.8.89	5	Salesman
NEW RECORDS - GROUP A					
ANOTHER APPOINTMENT					
Edwin Inchcliffe	Admin	1.1.76	4.4.89	13	Clerk
Leonard Winston	Sales	3.9.81	6.6.97	5	Ledger Clerk
EARLY RETIREMENT					
Keith Gladstone	Personnel	2.10.60	28.12.88	28	Personnel Manager
NEW RECORDS - GROUP B					
EARLY RETIREMENT					
Greta Maidstone	Marketing	14.2.86	16.3.89	3	Clerk
MATERNITY LEAVE					
Brenda Constant	Admin	9.9.75	6.5.89	13	Typist
ILL HEALTH					
Phillippa Cooper	Sales	8.6.56	12.10.89	33	Typist

TASK 3 *Section 1 – Objectives* 021, 022, 023, 024, 025, 026, 027, *028, *029

1 Load the Database program.

2 Set up a file for the centre sheets of woman's magazine. The recipes are intended to be cut out and saved. The field headings are as shown on Data Sheet 3 – these can be abbreviated if required. The filename used is RECIPES.

3 Use the following code letters:

In the FREEZE field:

Y = Yes
N = No

In the POWER LEVEL field:

L = Low
M = Medium
MH = Medium High
H = High

4 Enter the data as shown on Data Sheet 3. *Remember to proofread as fields are entered.*

5 Save the complete file.

6 Print a copy of the complete file.

7 Proofread and make any amendments before proceeding to the remainder of the Task.

8 Add the new records shown on Data Sheet 3 under NEW RECORDS – GROUP A.

9 Delete the recipe for Vegetable soup.

10 Make the following changes:

```
A reader has pointed out that the preparation time for
Wayfarer's Stew is nearer to 7 minutes than the 15
given.  Make the necessary correction.

If the Lasagne is cooked on a High setting, it goes
hard.  It is better cooked on a MH setting.  Change
the setting.
```

11 Sort the file into alphabetical order of NAME.

12 Save the file.

13 Print the complete file.

DATA SHEET 3 – DATABASES

NAME	NUMBER SERVED	PREPARATION TIME	COOK TIME	FREEZE	POWER LEVEL
Beef Stroganoff	6	15	21	Yes	Medium High
Wayfarer's Stew	6	15	45	Yes	Medium
Austrian Steak	4	10	70	Yes	Medium
Lasagne	8	15	38	No	High
Chocolate Mousse	8	10	8	No	High
Chocolate Cookies	4 doz	4	65	Yes	High
Vegetable Soup	8	20	60	No	Medium
Carrot Cake	8	10	15	No	High
Baked Potatoes	4	5	19	No	High
Baked Peach Melba	6	5	10	Yes	High
Spaghetti and Meatballs	6	12	47	Yes	Medium
Duck a l'Orange	4	5	56	No	High
NEW RECORDS - GROUP A					
Liver Pate	2	15	20	No	Medium
Rice Pudding	6	5	9	No	Medium High
NEW RECORDS - GROUP B					
Bread Pudding	5	10	42	Yes	Low
Chocolate Pudding	6	5	7	No	High

TASK 4 *Section 1 – Objectives* 021, 022, 023, 024, 025, 026, 027, *028, *029

1 Start up the system.

?

DO YOU KNOW?
What it means to format a disk?
How to format a disk?

2 Format a new disk.

3 Load the Database program.

4 Recall the file RECIPES.

?

DO YOU KNOW?
How to search records by a keyfield?
How to print the records found?

5 The recipes are to be cross-referenced for the freezer page of the magazine:

```
Search for the recipes which can be frozen.  Print all
fields for the records found.

Search for the recipes which cannot be frozen.  Print all
fields for the records found.

A reader has requested a list of recipes which serve more
than five.  Make the search and print all fields for the
records found.
```

6 Back up the file on to the newly formatted disk.

?

DO YOU KNOW?
How to search on more than one criterion?
How to print selected fields following a search?

7 The Editor has asked for some suggestions for recipes which will not take long to prepare and which can be frozen.

```
Make the search and print the list showing the name of the
recipe and the preparation time.

Search for the recipes which serve eight and are cooked on
High Power.  Print the name and the cooking time.
```

8 Add the new records (Group B) shown on Data Sheet 3 under NEW RECORDS – GROUP B.

9 Delete the record for Austrian Steak.

10 Save and print the complete file.

11 Delete the file RECIPES and any subsets of that file you may have created.

12 Delete the back-up file.

13 Close down the system.

TASK 5 *Section 1 – Objectives* 021, 022, 023, 024, 025, 026, 027, *028, *029

1 Start up the system and load a Database program.

2 Recall the file CRUISERS.

3 Practise searching by a keyfield, and either print a copy of the search as requested, or save as a subset and print later.

```
A customer has asked for a list of the cruisers which cost
below £50,000.  Find the records and print a copy of all
fields.

The Manager has been asked by a number of clients for
cruisers with less than five berths.  Find the records and
print a copy of the NAME and PRICE of each cruiser found.

Class B Cruisers are becoming increasingly popular, and it
would be useful to have a list of those available.  Find
the records and print them showing the NAME, OVERALL LENGTH
and BEAM.

The Cheetah range is to undergo a price revision.  Search
for all Cheetah models, and print a list showing NAME and
current PRICE.
```

4 Add the new records shown on Data Sheet 1 (Group B) under NEW RECORDS – GROUP A.

5 Delete the records for the Terrier 2876 and Cheetah 612.

? DO YOU KNOW?
How to print individual records?

6 Save the file and print a copy of the three added records.

7 Retain the file for use in Task 6.

? DO YOU KNOW?
How to send a message to another computer?

8 Using equipment available to you, and following the instructions given to you by your tutor, connect the computer to another source and send the following message:

CLAIT Database Exercises

I have now completed five of the Database exercises and am becoming more knowledgeable about the program.

Signed:

Date:

9 Close down the system.

TASK 6 *Section 1 – Objectives* 021, 022, 023, 024, 025, 026, 027, *028, *029

1 Start up the system and load a Database program.

2 Recall the file CRUISERS.

3 Sort the file into descending order of beam size.

4 Make the following amendments to the records:

```
There has been some internal restructuring of the Corgi 465
and it now has three berths.  Amend the record.

The price of the Bulldog 1100 has been reduced by £1,000.
Change the price field.
```

5 Make the following searches of the file:

```
Search for the Cheetah range of cruisers and print a
copy showing NAME and PRICE, for an interested
customer.

Search for those cruisers which cost over £75,000 and
which have more than two cabins.  Print showing NAME,
NO OF BERTHS and NO OF CABINS.

Search for those cruisers which have engines of more
than 250 hp and print all fields.
```

6 Save the file.

7 Print a copy of the amended records only.

8 Delete the file CRUISERS from the disk.

9 Close down the system.

TASK 7 *Section 1 – Objectives* 021, 022, 023, 024, 025, 026, 027, *028, *029

1 Start up the system and load a Database program.

2 Recall the file LEAVERS.

3 Make the following searches:

```
The Personnel Manager would like a list of the staff who
have taken Maternity Leave.  Search for the staff and print
all fields.

The Sales Director would like a list of the staff who have
left his Department with 15 or more years of service.
Print the list showing the NAME and YEARS OF SERVICE only.

A number of staff left to take up other employment.  Search
for these and print a copy showing the NAME and DEPARTMENT
only.
```

4 Add the new records shown on Data Sheet 2 under NEW RECORDS – GROUP B. These employees left during 1989.

5 Print a copy of the three added records.

6 Make the following changes to the file:

```
Joanne Coleman who took maternity leave did, in fact,
return to work full time.  Her record should therefore be
deleted from the file.

Brian Stanton of Administration was a Clerical Officer.
His record shows Clerical Assistant.  Make the necessary
change.  Print a copy of the amended record.
```

7 Save the file and print a copy of the complete file.

8 Delete the file LEAVERS and any subsets you may have created from the disk.

9 Connect the computer to another system and send the following message:

CLAIT Database Exercises

Make up a message of approximately 50 words saying what you have learned up to this point.

Signed:

Date:

10 Close down the system.

Section 1 – Objectives 021, 022, 023, 024, 025, 026, 027, *028, *029

?

DO YOU REMEMBER?

How to set up a database file?

How to add records?

How to delete records?

How to amend records?

How to sort records?

How to search for specified records?

How to print a file?

How to print a record?

Note: The following exercises give plent of practice on the above.

TASK 8

1 Power up the system and format a blank disk.

2 Load the Database program.

3 Set up a file containing information on video cameras. Use the filename CAMERAS. Use the following field titles, which can be sensibly abbreviated if necessary:

```
MODEL
PRICE
HOW HELD
ZOOM RATIO
APERTURE
AUTO FOCUS
LENS LENGTH
```

Use the following code letters:

```
In the AUTOFOCUS field        Y  =  YES
                              N  =  NO

In the HOW HELD field         H  =  HAND
                              S  =  SHOULDER
```

4 Input the data as given on Data Sheet 4.

Make sure code letters are used. If they are not, they count as data entry errors. For example, if no codes are used in this task, you will be penalised for four data entry errors, and therefore Profile Sentence 022 cannot be awarded.

DATA SHEET 4 – DATABASES

MODEL	PRICE	HOW HELD	ZOOM RATIO	APERTURE	AUTO FOCUS	LENS LENGTH	STOCK
P279	625	Hand	8:1	F1.2	Yes	9-75	4
KL100	719	Shoulder	12:1	F1.2	Yes	9-75	5
KL101	615	Shoulder	12:1	F1.4	No	3-2	3
KL110	890	Hand	10:1	F1.4	No	12-72	6
KL256	900	Hand	6:1	F1.6	Yes	12-72	4
P511	799	Shoulder	10:1	F1.2	Yes	8-80	4
P716	650	Shoulder	8:1	F1.4	Yes	12-72	3
P331	699	Hand	6:1	F1.6	No	9-54	4
T216	810	Shoulder	10:1	F1.6	Yes	11-88	1
T469	750	Hand	12:1	F1.4	Yes	9-75	7
T716	675	Hand	8:1	F1.4	No	11-88	4
V800	599	Shoulder	8:1	F1.2	No	11-88	2
V801	899	Hand	6:1	F1.2	Yes	9-54	3
R176	900	Shoulder	12:1	F1.4	No	12-72	1
R276	575	Shoulder	10:1	F1.4	No	8-80	6
D200	799	Shoulder	6:1	F1.6	No	9-54	8
D202	825	Shoulder	6:1	F1.6	Yes	8-80	3
NEW RECORDS - GROUP A							
B659	415	Hand	8:1	F1.2	Yes	9-75	10
B660	650	Shoulder	10:1	F1.2	No	3-2	9
B427	500	Shoulder	6:1	F1.4	No	12-72	6
NEW RECORDS - GROUP B							
B724	499	Hand	12:1	F1.6	Yes	9-75	4
NEW RECORDS - GROUP C							
P411	875	Hand	6:1	F1.4	Yes	11-88	6
P511	599	Shoulder	8:1	F1.6	No	12-72	6

5 Save the file using the filename CAMERAS.

6 Load the printer with paper, set to top of form and print the complete file.

7 Recall the file CAMERAS and make the following amendments:

```
The price of the KL256 has been reduced by £150 - correct
the record.

Three new cameras have been received, add them to the
stock.  The data is shown on Data Sheet 4 under NEW RECORDS
- GROUP A.

The last of the T216 cameras have been sold.  It cannot be
restocked, therefore the record should be deleted from the
file.

The camera Model R176 is very expensive at £900 - for what
it does.  Reduce the price by £250 to try and sell the one
we have in stock quickly.

A new camera has been received.  Add the record to the
file, the data is shown on Data Sheet 4 under NEW RECORDS -
GROUP B.

Camera Model D202 does not have Auto Focus as indicated.
Please amend the record.
```

8 The following information is required and must be found either by sorting or by searching:

```
Sort the file into ascending order of price.  Print all
fields of the sorted file.

A customer has asked for details of the Auto Focus cameras
in stock.  Carry out a search for them and print all
fields.

Looking around the shop, I note that the stock of some
cameras is getting low.  Find all the cameras with less
than four in stock and print out MODEL, PRICE and STOCK.

Search for cameras in stock which have an APERTURE of F1.2
and a LENS LENGTH of 9-75.  Print MODEL and STOCK.
```

9 R176 has sold quickly at the new price, as this is the last of the stock I do not intend reordering. Delete the record from the file.

10 Save and print the complete file.

11 Back-up the file.

Section 1 – Objectives 021, 022, 023, 024, 025, 026, 027, *028, *029

TASK 9

1 Recall the file called CAMERAS.

2 Add the records to the file for the two new cameras which have been added to the stock. The details are on Data Sheet 4 under NEW RECORDS – GROUP C.

3 Print the new records only.

4 The following price changes have to be made. Amend the records as necessary.

```
B724 increased by £25
KL101 reduced by £35
D202 reduced by £75
```

5 There have been revised specifications for three of the cameras held in stock. Make the necessary amendments to the records:

```
P511 has Auto Focus
B427 has a Zoom Ratio of 10:1
T716 is now Shoulder held
```

6 Make the following searches:

```
A special request has been received from a customer for a
list of cameras with a Zoom Ratio of 1:6 below £600.  Find
the cameras and print all fields.

List all cameras below £700 with less than five in stock.
Print MODEL and PRICE only.
```

7 Save the file.

8 Print the complete file.

9 Delete the original and the back-up copy of CAMERAS and any subsets created.

10 Connect the computer to another source and send the following message:

CLAIT Database Tasks

Send a message of approximately 50 words explaining what a Database is, to a friend who does not know. Your explanation should include the terms FILE, RECORD, FIELD, SORT and SEARCH.

Signed:

Date:

11 Close down the system.

Section 1 – Objectives 021, 022, 023, 024, 025, 026, 027, *029, *030

?

DO YOU REMEMBER?

Check Task 8 for the things you need to remember.

TASK 10

1 Start up the system and format a disk.

2 Load the Database program.

3 Set up a file showing the holidays available during June and July. Use the following field headings, which may be abbreviated if necessary. Use the filename HOLIDAYS.

```
DATE
DESTINATION
HOLIDAY REF
NO OF NIGHTS
ACCOMMODATION (1)
ACCOMMODATION (2)
DEPARTURE AIRPORT
PRICE
FLIGHT ONLY
```

Use the following code letters:

```
In the ACCOMMODATION (2) field   AO = Accommodation Only
                                 BB = Bed and Breakfast
                                 HB = Half Board
                                 FB = Full Board

In the DEPARTURE AIRPORT field   B  = Birmingham
                                 E  = East Midlands
                                 M  = Manchester
```

Dates should be keyed in as MONTH and DAY, eg JUNE 20

4 Enter the data as given on Data Sheet 5.

5 Save the file.

6 Put paper into the printer, set paper to top of form and print the complete file.

7 *Do not delete this file from the disk until told to do so.*

8 Recall the file HOLIDAYS.

9 Three new holidays have become available. Add the records to the files. The data is given on Data Sheet 5 under NEW RECORDS – GROUP A.

10 Print the new records only.

DATA SHEET 5 – DATABASES

DATE	DESTINATION	HOLIDAY REF	NO OF NIGHTS	ACCOMMODATION (1)	DEPARTURE AIRPORT	PRICE	FLIGHT ONLY
ACCOMMODATION ONLY							
June 20	Cyprus	T761	14	Apartment	Birmingham	225	n/a
July 4	Crete	T769	7	Apartment	Birmingham	225	129
July 21	Corfu	T777	14	Apartment	Manchester	235	99
July 10	Ibiza	T768	14	Apartment	Birmingham	209	99
June 20	Majorca	T773	14	Apartment	Manchester	235	99
June 20	Algarve	T776	14	Apartment	Birmingham	219	119
June 27	Tenerife	T770	14	Apartment	East Midlands	279	149
July 4	Costa del Sol	T763	11	Apartment	Manchester	269	159
June 27	Costa Dorada	T767	14	Apartment	Birmingham	179	69
BED AND BREAKFAST							
June 27	Austrian Tyrol	T762	7	Hotel	Manchester	149	49
July 4	Rhodes	T778	12	Hotel	East Midlands	229	159
July 4	Austrian Tyrol	T764	14	Hotel	Manchester	299	99
FULL BOARD							
July 4	Paris	T782	10	Hotel	Manchester	200	55
June 20	Norway	T771	14	Hotel	Manchester	229	109
HALF BOARD							
June 20	Ibiza	T779	10	Hotel	Birmingham	159	69
July 15	Greece	T775	14	Hotel	East Midlands	250	109
July 15	Costa Almeria	T781	10	Hotel	Manchester	245	119
NEW RECORDS - GROUP A							
ACCOMMODATION ONLY							
July 8	Yugoslavia	T780	12	Apartment	Manchester	300	n/a
FULL BOARD							
July 11	Rome	T766	10	Hotel	Birmingham	225	79
HALF BOARD							
June 14	Turin	T783	14	Hotel	East Midlands	270	80
NEW RECORDS - GROUP B							
ACCOMMODATION ONLY							
July 10	Canaries	T772	12	Apartment	Manchester	250	n/a
BED AND BREAKFAST							
July 1	Malaga	T774	10	Hotel	Birmingham	210	75
HALF BOARD							
June 14	Jersey	T765	8	Hotel	East Midlands	270	80

11 The following information is required and needs to be printed out. Find the information by sorting or searching the file.

```
Sort the file into ascending numerical order of REFERENCE.
Print all fields of the sorted file.

Search for the holidays which depart from Birmingham
Airport and print all fields.

Sort the file into descending order of PRICE.  Print all
fields of the sorted file.
```

12 Make the following amendments to the file:

```
The holiday to Paris, REF T782, is now full and the record
should be deleted from the file.

The price of the holiday to Majorca on 20th June, REF T773
has been reduced by £20 on the full price and by £5 on the
Flight Only price.

Holiday REF T780 is now available on a Flight Only basis at
a cost of £100.
```

13 Save the file.

14 Connect the computer to another source and send the following message:

CLAIT Database Tasks

The holidays given in the Database are all currently available at the prices shown and on the dates given. You may book any holiday by calling in at our offices.

Signed:

Date:

15 Close down the system.

Section 1 – Objectives 021, 022, 023, 024, 025, 026, 027, *028, *029

TASK 11

1 Start up the system and load the Database package.

2 Recall the file HOLIDAYS.

3 The following holidays have been altered in price. Change the records as necessary:

```
T764     reduced by £25
T775     reduced by £25
T765     increased by £10
```

4 The manager has asked for details of holidays as given below. Make the necessary searches to find the information, and print as indicated.

```
Search for the holidays which are available on an accommo-
dation only basis and print DESTINATION and PRICE for each
one.

Search for holidays from Manchester which are on an apart-
ment only basis.  Print DATE and DESTINATION.

Search for holidays which are for 14 nights and print all
fields.
```

5 Three new holidays have become available. Add the records to the file. The data is given on Data Sheet 5 under NEW RECORDS – GROUP B.

6 The date is now 23rd June, therefore the files for the holidays for 20th June should be deleted from the file.

7 Carry out the following sort:

```
Sort the records into ascending alphabetical order of
DESTINATION.  Save and print the sorted file.
```

8 Delete the file from the disk.

9 Connect the computer to another source and send the following message:

CLAIT Database Tasks

To: My Tutor

From: (insert your name)

I have now completed all the tasks in the Database Section and I am ready to proceed to the Assignments.

Signed:

Date:

10 Shut down the system.

Assignment 1—Databases

Section 1 – Objectives 021, 022, 023, 024, 025, 026, 027, 028*, 029*

Section 2 – Objectives 056, 057, 058, 059, 060, 061, 062, 063, 064, 065, 066, 067, 071

1 Power up the system.

2 Format a blank disk *or* select an empty user area.

3 Load a Database program and set up a file giving details of courses offered by the Secretarial Section of Hometown College of FE. Use the following field titles and abbreviate if necessary. Use the filename COURSES.

```
SUBJECT
LOCATION
DURATION
DAY
CLASS TIMES
COMMENCING
CONTACT
```

Use the following code letters:

In the CLASS TIMES field	A	5.00 - 7.00
	B	6.00 - 8.00
	C	6.00 - 9.00
	D	6.30 - 8.30
	E	7.00 - 9.00
In the COMMENCING field	11	110989
	12	120989
	13	130989
	14	140989

4 Enter the data given on Assignment 1 – Data Sheet.

Make sure code letters are used for CLASS TIMES and COMMENCING.

5 Load the printer with paper which is set to top of form and print out the complete file.

6 The CLASS TIMES for CLAIT have been given incorrectly. They should be 6.30–8.30. Change the record.

7 There have been so many applications for Stage I Word Processing and Stage I Typewriting, that an additional class has been provided in each subject. Add new records as given in the NEW RECORDS section of Assignment 1 – Data Sheet.

8 There have been so few enrolments for Advanced Shorthand that the class has been cancelled. Delete the record.

9 Sort and print the complete file in *alphabetical* order of SUBJECT.

10 Save the sorted file and copy it on to the newly formatted disk.

11 Recall the file COURSES.

12 Search the file for all those subjects in the Word Processing category and print out all the information for each of these records.

13 Find all the classes in the Typewriting Skills Stage II category and print out DURATION and CLASS TIMES.

14 Save the data and check the directory to make sure it has been saved.

15 Delete the back-up file from the disk.

16 Close down the system.

17 Connect the computer to another source and send the following message:

TO: CLAIT Tutor

From: (your name)

I have completed this first practise Database Assignment on (insert today's date) and hope I would have passed.

ASSIGNMENT 1 – DATA SHEET

SUBJECT	DURATION	DAY	CLASS TIMES	COMMENCING	CONTACT
COLLEGE					
Word Processing II Pt I	12	Wednesday	5.00 - 7.00	13/09/89	Jennifer Kelsey
Word Processing II Pt II	12	Wednesday	7.00 - 9.00	13/09/89	Jennifer Kelsey
Shorthand Beginners	15	Monday	6.00 - 8.00	11/09/89	Marilyn Summers
Word Processing III Pt I	12	Thursday	5.00 - 7.00	14/09/89	Jennifer Kelsey
Typewriting I	20	Monday	6.30 - 8.30	11/09/89	Felicity Andrews
Word Processing III Pt II	12	Thursday	7.00 - 9.00	14/09/89	Jennifer Kelsey
Word Processing I	12	Monday	6.30 - 8.30	11/09/89	Jennifer Kelsey
Shorthand Advanced	15	Tuesday	6.30 - 8.30	12/09/89	Marilyn Summers
NORTH ANNEXE					
CLAIT	36	Tuesday	6.00 - 9.00	12/09/89	Freda Alexander
Information Technology II	36	Wednesday	6.00 - 9.00	13/09/89	Freda Alexander
Typewriting II Pt I	20	Tuesday	6.30 - 8.30	12/09/89	Felicity Andrews
Typewriting II Pt II	20	Wednesday	6.30 - 8.30	13/09/89	Felicity Andrews
SOUTH ANNEXE					
Audio Typewriting	12	Monday	6.30 - 8.30	11/09/89	Joan Johnson
Shorthand Intermediate	15	Wednesday	6.00 - 8.00	13/09/89	Marilyn Summers
Typewriting III Pt I	20	Tuesday	6.30 - 8.30	12/09/89	Felicity Andrews
Typewriting III Pt II	20	Wednesday	6.30 - 8.30	13/09/89	Felicity Andrews
NEW RECORDS					
COLLEGE					
Word Processing I	12	Tuesday	6.30 - 8.30	12/09/89	Marilyn Summers
Typewriting I	20	Thursday	6.30 - 8.30	14/09/89	Felicity Andrews

Assignment 2—Databases

Section 1 – Objectives 021, 022, 023, 024, 025, 026, 027, 028*, 029*

Section 2 – Objectives 056, 057, 058, 059, 060, 061, 062, 063, 064, 065, 066, 067, 071

1 Power up the system.

2 Format a blank disk *or* select an empty user area.

3 Load a Database program and set up a file for the Wages Section of the Personnel Department. Use the following field titles, sensibly abbreviated if necessary:

```
EMPLOYEE NO
NAME
DEPARTMENT
NI NUMBER
TAX CODE
PAY METHOD
HOURLY RATE
```

In the NAME field type the name as shown on Assignment 2 – Data Sheet.

Use the following code letters:

In the PAY METHOD field	BO	BANKERS ORDER
	CA	CASH
	CH	CHEQUE
In the DEPARTMENT field	MAR	MARKETING
	SAL	SALES
	PER	PERSONNEL
	PRO	PRODUCTION

4 Enter the data given on Assignment 2 – Data Sheet.

Make sure code letters are used in the PAY METHOD and DEPARTMENT fields.

5 Load the printer with paper, set to top of form and print out the complete file.

6 Katherine Andrews has left the firm. Delete her record.

7 Brenda Antrobus has moved from PRODUCTION to PERSONNEL. Amend her record.

8 Two new members of staff have been employed. Amend the file using the data under the NEW RECORDS heading of the Assignment 2 – Data Sheet.

9 Sort and print the complete file in *ascending* numerical order of EMPLOYEE NO.

10 Search the file for all staff in the MARKETING Department. Print all the information for these records.

11 Find all the members of staff in the PERSONNEL Department who are paid by Bankers Order. Print the EMPLOYEE NO and NAME only.

12 Save the file.

13 List the directory on the screen and check that the file has been saved.

14 Copy the file on to the newly formatted disk *or* into the empty user area.

15 Delete the original file.

16 Connect the computer to another source and send the following message:

CLAIT Database Assignments

To: CLAIT Tutor

From: (insert your name)

Message: I have now finished the second Database assignment. Please tell me whether I would have passed if it had been the final assignment.

17 Close down the system.

ASSIGNMENT 2 – DATA SHEET

EMPLOYEE NO	NAME	NI NUMBER	TAX CODE	PAY METHOD	HOURLY RATE
MARKETING					
369	ANDREWS, KATHERINE	LR412326F	210L	CHEQUE	2.10
622	STEWART, PHYLLIS	AL396645F	210L	CASH	2.20
625	MOSS, JOHN	AP936654M	300L	CASH	2.70
767	CAREY, PHILIP	CV635649M	276H	BANKERS ORDER	3.00
PERSONNEL					
765	EVANS, PETER	PF263241M	261L	CASH	3.00
485	BROWN, BRIAN	PT173981M	315L	BANKERS ORDER	2.90
350	CARTWRIGHT, NIGEL	TJ155189M	310L	CHEQUE	3.00
679	HENSTOCK, ELIZABETH	LV511598F	210L	BANKERS ORDER	2.20
PRODUCTION					
414	HARTLEY, IAN	DP366594M	420H	CHEQUE	2.90
453	GREIG, LIAM	KV769231M	375H	BANKERS ORDER	3.00
322	ANTROBUS, BRENDA	PD672913F	210L	CASH	2.20
SALES					
421	GRAY, ADAM	TN622314M	279L	CASH	2.90
692	BUCKLEY, GERALD	PR234567M	280L	BANKERS ORDER	3.00
452	CRAIG, RUBY	LM325476F	210L	CHEQUE	2.70
399	ANDERTON, KEITH	NR472636M	250L	CHEQUE	3.00
NEW RECORDS					
MARKETING					
398	PRINGLE, DAVID	AO745263M	290L	CASH	2.70
PRODUCTION					
311	SMITH, ANTHONY	KR719318M	310H	CHEQUE	3.00

5 Graphics

Pie charts

Section 1 – Objectives 051, 054

Section 2 – Objectives 056, 057, 058, 059, 060, 061, 062, 063

?

DO YOU KNOW?

What a *pie chart* is?

What a pie chart represents?

What the total of all the segments represents?

How to put a main heading on a pie chart?

How to label the segments?

How to print a pie chart?

TASK 1

1 Load and run the program to be used for pie charts.

2 The chart will show the sales of electrical equipment for Astra Supplies Ltd for the month of June.

3 Generate a pie chart using the following values:

```
TVs        22
Videos     19
CDs        35
```

4 The main heading for the chart is JUNE SALES and you should include appropriate labels for each segment.

5 Print the pie chart.

The following tasks are each concerned with pie charts – follow the instructions for Task 1.

TASK 2

The pie chart represents languages taken by 6th Formers at Hometown Sixth Form College.

Chart heading – LANGUAGES.

Segment headings – use appropriate headings.

```
French     21
German     15
Spanish     6
Others      2
```

TASK 3

The pie chart represents video films sold during November by Hometown Video Stores.

Chart heading – VIDEO SALES.

Segment headings – use appropriate headings.

Crime	35
Sport	14
Travel	10
Romance	29

TASK 4 The pie chart represents the number of different types of printer in Hometown College of FE.

Chart heading – PRINTERS.

Segment headings – use appropriate headings.

Daisywheels	5
Dot Matrix	37
Laser	3
Other	2

TASK 5 The pie chart represents the sales of caravans by Astra Caravan Sales during the quarter ended 30th June.

Chart heading – CARAVAN SALES.

Segment headings – use appropriate headings.

Cheetah	15
Tiger	19
Puma	26
Lion	4

Line graphs

Section 1 – Objectives 053, 054

Section 2 – Objectives 056, 057, 058, 059, 060, 061, 062, 063

?

DO YOU KNOW?

What a *line graph* is?

What does it represent?

Which is the X axis?

Which is the Y axis?

How to plot the points on a line graph?

How to print a line graph?

TASK 6

1 Load and run the program to be used for line graphs.

2 The graph will show the lending figures for the loans of books on travel from the mobile library for January to June.

3 Generate a line graph using the following data:

January	97
February	62
March	53
April	71
May	67
June	58

4 Label the graph as follows:

X axis (horizontal) – MONTHS
Y axis (vertical) – LOANS

5 Graph heading – MOBILE LIBRARY LOANS(1)

6 Print the line graph.

The following tasks are each concerned with line graphs – follow the instructions given for Task 6.

TASK 7

The line graph represents the numbers of pupils in the 6th form of Hometown Sixth Form College from 1984–89.

Generate a line graph using the following data:

1984	15
1985	21
1986	26
1987	20
1988	30
1989	25

Label the graph as follows:

X axis – YEAR
Y axis – PUPILS

Graph heading – 6TH FORM STATISTICS(1)

Print the line graph.

TASK 8

The graph shows the number of tennis matches played by players A to F for Homeshire County during the summer season.

Generate a line graph using the following data:

A	19
B	3
C	12
D	8
E	14
F	21

Label the graph as follows:

X axis – PLAYER
Y axis – NO OF MATCHES

Graph heading – TENNIS MATCHES(1)

Print the line graph.

TASK 9

The graph shows the number of houses sold by the Hometown Estate Agents during July to December.

Generate a line graph using the following data:

July	62
August	44
September	59
October	52
November	35
December	24

Label the graph as follows:

X axis – MONTH
Y axis – NO OF HOUSES

Graph heading – HOUSE SALES(1)

Print the line graph.

TASK 10 The graph shows the Tuck Shop takings for Hometown Comprehensive School for the period September to March in pounds.

Generate a line graph using the following data:

September	39
October	30
November	38
December	26
January	20
February	40
March	31

Label the graph as follows:

X axis – MONTH
Y axis – TAKINGS (in £s)

Graph heading – TUCK SHOP TAKINGS(1)

Print the line graph.

Bar charts/histograms

Section 1 – Objectives 052, 054

Section 2 – Objectives 056, 057, 058, 059, 060, 061, 062, 063

?

DO YOU KNOW?

What a *bar chart* or *histogram* is?

What does it represent?

Which is the X axis?

Which is the Y axis?

How to enter the headings for each value?

How to put a title to a bar chart?

How to print a bar chart?

TASK 11

1 Using the following data draw a bar chart/histogram:

January	97
February	62
March	53
April	71
May	67
June	58

2 Label the bar chart as follows:

X axis (horizontal) MONTHS
Y axis (vertical) LOANS

3 Enter suitable headings for each bar using abbreviations if necessary.

4 Chart heading – MOBILE LIBRARY LOANS(2).

5 Print the bar chart.

The following tasks are each concerned with charts/histograms – follow the instructions given for Task 12.

TASK 12 The bar chart uses the same data and headings as Task 8.

Chart heading – 6TH FORM STATISTICS(2)

TASK 13 The bar chart uses the same data and headings as Task 9.

Chart heading – TENNIS MATCHES(2)

TASK 14 The bar chart uses the same data and headings as Task 10.

Chart heading – HOUSE SALES(2)

TASK 15 The bar chart uses the same data and headings as Task 11.

Chart heading – TUCK SHOP TAKINGS(2)

Graphs using formulae

Section 1 – Objectives 055, 054

Section 2 – Objectives 056, 057, 058, 059, 060, 061, 062, 063

? DO YOU KNOW?
How to plot a graph using a formula?
How to print the graph using a formula?

TASK 16

1 Load and run the graph program which can use a formula.

2 Name the horizontal axis GALLONS and the vertical axis LITRES.

3 Set the graph to display from 0 to 150 litres and 0 to 25 gallons.

4 Input the formula $Y = 4.54 \times X$ or any appropriate formula to convert gallons to litres.

5 Print the graph.

6 Close down the system.

The following tasks are for graphs which can use formulae – follow the instructions for Task 17.

TASK 17

1 Name the horizontal axis MPG and the vertical axis KPL.

2 Set the graph to display from 0 to 20 KPL and 0 to 50 MPG.

3 Input the formula $Y = 0.35 \times X$ or any appropriate formula to convert miles per gallon to kilometres per litre.

TASK 18

1 Name the horizontal axis FEET and the vertical axis FATHOMS.

2 Set the graph to display from 0 to 15 fathoms and 0 to 80 feet.

3 Input the formula Y = X/6 or any appropriate formula to convert feet to fathoms.

TASK 19

1 Name the horizontal axis HECTARES and the vertical axis ACRES.

2 Set the graph to display from 0 to 500 acres and 0 to 200 hectares.

3 Input the formula Y = 2.47 × X or any appropriate formula to convert hectares to acres.

TASK 20

1 Name the horizontal axis HOURS and the vertical axis DAYS.

2 Set the graph to display from 0 to 15 days and 0 to 400 hours.

3 Input the formula Y = X/24 or any appropriate formula to convert hours to days.

Drawing programs

Section 1 – Objectives 046, 047, 048, 049, 050

Section 2 – Objectives 056, 057, 058, 059, 060, 061, 062, 063

?

DO YOU KNOW?

What you can do with a drawing program?

How to draw an outline of a given plan?

How to draw shapes and symbols?

How to change shapes and symbols?

How to store shapes and symbols?

How to colour or shade sections?

How to label the drawings with text?

TASK 21

1 Load a program which allows you to draw shapes.

2 The outline below shows a small car park at the back of a building. Draw the outline as shown:

3 Divide the longest wall at the top and the bottom into six equal car parking spaces.

4 Position a rectangle in three of the spaces to represent cars.

5 Shade the rectangles.

6 Print the finished plan.

TASK 22

1 Load a program which allows you to draw shapes.

2 The outline below shows a self-service store. Draw the outline as shown including the text:

3 There are to be shelves around three sides of the walls. Work out a suitable shape and position the shelves.

4 In addition, there are to be three free-standing shelves in the middle of the shop. Draw a rectangle to represent the shelves, save the shape and copy it into the outline in a reasonable position.

5 At the entrance there are three checkouts. Draw a circle to represent the checkouts, save the shape and copy it into the outline.

6 Save and print the plan.

7 Change the circles for the checkout to squares.

8 Shade the checkout squares.

9 Print out the finished plan.

TASK 23

1 Load a program which allows you to draw shapes.

2 The outline shown below is the sales area and fitting rooms of a knitwear shop. Draw the outline as shown, including text.

3 Position the following into the sales area:

- 2 circular stands for knitwear
- 2 long thin rectangles for rails – one for jackets, the other for trousers
- a rectangle for the pay desk near the entrance

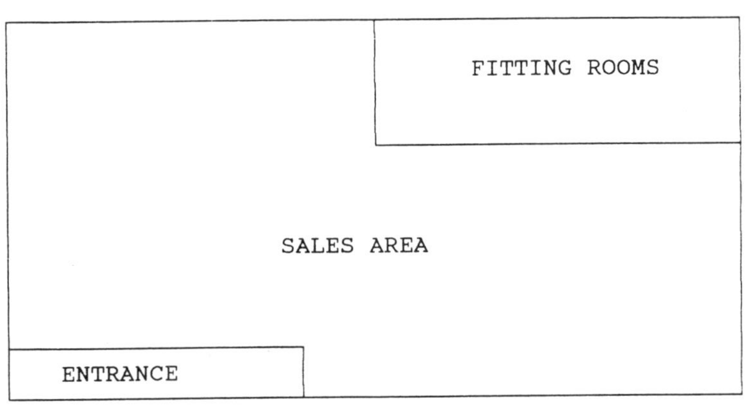

4 Divide the fitting room into three separate cubicles.

5 Save and print the plan.

6 Replace one of the circular stands with a square stand.

7 Shade the rectangles representing rails.

8 Print the finished plan.

9 Shut down the system.

TASK 24

1 Load the program for drawing shapes.

2 The outline below shows the reception area of the offices of Hometown Chemicals. Draw the outline as shown, including the text.

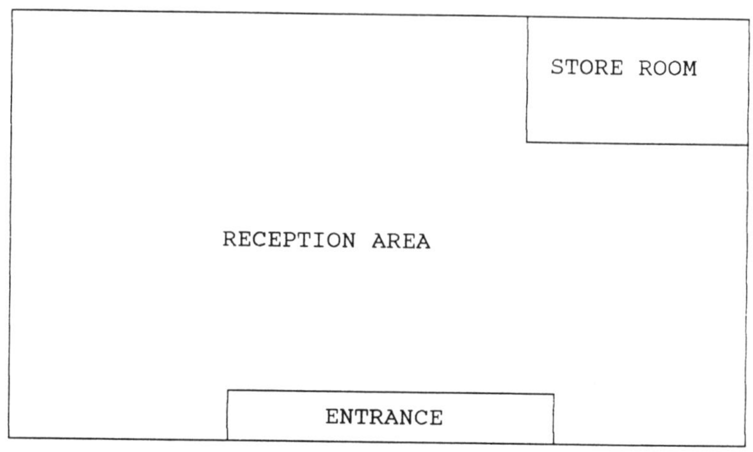

3 Position the following into the reception area:

- square for desk
- square for table
- three half-circles for visitors' chairs

4 Inside each table square put another square representing a fax machine and a photocopier.

5 Save and print the plan.

6 Recall the plan and make the following changes:

- replace the circular coffee table with a square table
- shade the squares representing the fax and the photocopier

7 Save and print the amended plan.

8 Shut down the system.

TASK 25

1 Load the program for drawing shapes.

2 The outline shown below is for a small exhibition hall. Draw the outline as shown including the text:

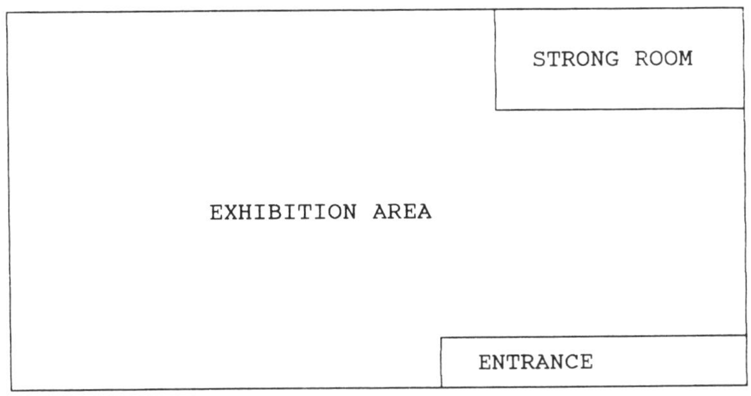

3 Position the following into the exhibition area:

- a square desk at the entrance for handing out tickets
- four rectangles around the edges of the exhibition area for glass cases
- two circular stands in the centre

4 Save and print the plan.

5 Recall the plan and make the following amendments:

- replace one of the circular stands with a square stand
- shade the desk

6 Save and print the revised plan.

Assignment 1—Graphics

Section 1 – Objectives 046, 047, 048, 049, 050, 051, 052, 053, 054, *055

Section 2 – Objectives 057, 060, 062, 063

PART 1

1 Load a program which allows the drawing of shapes.

2 Draw the outline of the plan as given below, including the text:

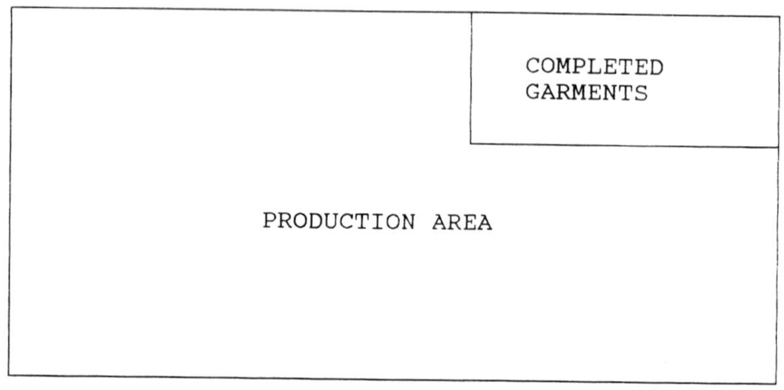

3 The production area has three rectangular benches. Design the outline shape of the bench and store it. Put the three rectangular benches in position.

4 A square cutting-out table needs to be positioned in the production area.

5 Put a square on each bench to represent a sewing machine.

6 Put a square in the area marked 'completed garments'.

7 Save the plan and print a copy.

8 Shade the squares which represent the sewing machines.

9 Change the square in the area marked 'completed garments' to a circle and shade it.

10 Save and print the amended plan.

PART 2

11 Load and run a graph program which will allow you to draw a pie chart to display the proportions which make up the cost of an item.

12 Generate a pie chart using the following data:

Cost Price	76
Selling Price	112
Profit	36

13 Name the pie chart PROFIT and include suitable labels for each of the segments.

14 Print the pie chart.

15 Load and run a graph program which will generate a bar chart/histogram. The graph will show the total sales of stationery items from the College Shop during the month of September.

16 Name the X axis (horizontal) ITEMS and the Y axis (vertical) NUMBER.

17 Produce the bar chart/histogram using the following data:

PENS	62
PENCILS	101
RIBBONS	22
RUBBERS	35
RULERS	26
STAPLES	20

18 Put in the appropriate headings, using sensible abbreviations where necessary.

19 The title of the bar chart/histogram is STATIONERY SALES.

20 Print the bar chart/histogram.

21 Load a program which can be used to produce a line graph.

22 Name the X axis ITEMS and the Y axis NUMBER.

23 Using the data given in stage 17 above, plot and generate a line graph.

24 Enter the headings for each item, and use the name STATIONERY SALES(2).

25 Print the line graph.

26 Load and run a graph program which will enable you to generate a graph using a formula.

27 Name the horizontal axis MINUTES and the vertical axis HOURS.

28 Set the graph to display from 0 to 25 hours and 0 to 1500 minutes.

29 Input the formula Y = X/60 or a suitable formula to convert minutes to hours.

30 Print the graph.

31 Close down the system.

Assignment 2—Graphics

PART 1

Section 1 – Objectives 046, 047, 048, 049, 050, 051, 052, 053, 054, *055

Section 2 – Objectives 057, 060, 062, 063

1 Load a program which allows the drawing of shapes.

2 Draw the outline plan as given below, including the text:

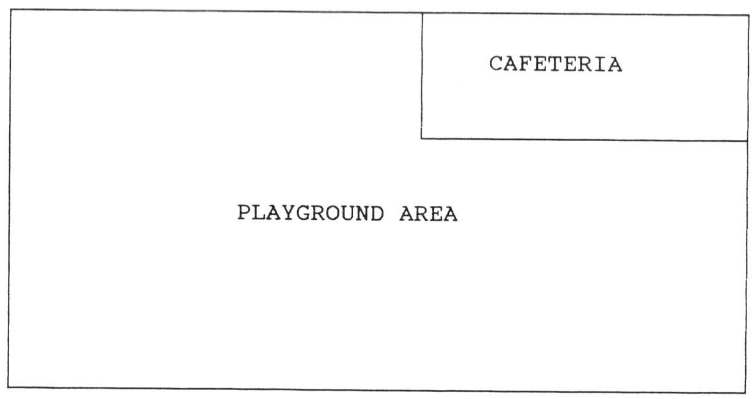

3 The Playground area has two squares for swings. Design the outline shape of the swing and store it. Put the two swings into position.

4 The following other play items also need to be positioned – a square for a sandpit, a rectangle for a slide and a circle for a roundabout. Design the outline shapes and put them into position.

5 Put a small circle in the Cafeteria area to represent the counter.

6 Save the plan and print a copy.

7 Shade the squares for the swings.

8 Change the square sandpit and make it a circular one. Shade it.

9 Save and print the amended plan.

PART 2

10 Load and run a graph program which will allow you to draw a pie chart to display the costs of Astra Manufacturing Co in thousands of pounds during 1989.

11 Generate a pie chart using the following data:

Raw Materials	27
Labour	49
Overheads	36

12 Name the chart COSTS and include suitable headings for each of the segments.

13 Print the pie chart.

14 Load and run a graph program which will produce a bar chart/histogram. The graph will show the software packages sold by Astra Computing during April.

15 Name the X axis (horizontal) PACKAGE and the Y axis (vertical) NUMBER SOLD.

16 Produce the bar chart/histogram using the following data:

WORD PROCESSING	24
SPREADSHEETS	20
DATABASES	16
GRAPHICS	10
VIEWDATA	5
DESK TOP PUBLISHING	25

17 Put in the appropriate headings, using sensible abbreviations where necessary.

18 The title of the bar chart/histogram is SOFTWARE SALES.

19 Print the bar chart/histogram.

20 Load a program which can produce a line graph.

21 Name the X axis PACKAGE and the Y axis NUMBER SOLD.

22 Using the data given in stage 16 above, produce a line graph.

23 Enter the headings for each item and use the name SOFTWARE SALES(2).

24 Print the line graph.

25 Load and run a graph program which will enable you to produce a graph using a formula.

26 Name the horizontal axis YARDS and the vertical axis METRES.

27 Set the graph to display from 0 to 20 yards and 0 to 20 metres.

28 Input the formula $Y = X \times 0.91$ or a suitable formula to convert yards to metres.

29 Print the graph.

30 Close down the system.

6 Stock control

?

DO YOU KNOW?

How to start up the system?

How to load a *stock control* program?

What is meant by stock control?

Why is it necessary?

How to set up a *stock record*?

What is meant by *stock level*?

What is meant by *minimum level*?

What is meant by *reorder quantity*?

TASK 1

1 Start up the system and load a stock control program.

2 Enter the data for the stock items on Stock Control – Data Sheet 1.

?

DO YOU KNOW?

How to load the printer with paper?

How to set the printer to 'top of form'?

How to print the stock list?

How to print a report showing items which need reordering?

3 Load the printer, set to top of form and print the complete stock list.

4 Print a summary report showing items which need reordering.

?

DO YOU KNOW?

How to add stock items?

How to amend stock items?

How to delete stock items?

5 Add the two new stock items shown on Data Sheet 1 – NEW RECORDS – 5.

6 The manufacturers have increased the price of E176 by 50p. Make this change to the record.

7 M101 is not selling well, decrease the price by £1.00. Make this change to the record.

8 Print the complete revised stock list.

DATA SHEET 1 – STOCK CONTROL

REF	DESCRIPTION	UNIT	VALUE £	STOCK LEVEL	MINIMUM LEVEL	REORDER QUANTITY
K299	Suspension Files	50	15.95	16	10	20
T275	A4 White Copier Paper	Ream	2.95	25	40	100
E176	DL Envelopes	1000	25.00	31	20	45
E186	C6 Envelopes	1000	19.99	21	20	45
E196	C4 Envelopes	250	25.99	15	20	45
M101	Stapler	Single	6.95	6	5	5
M123	Post It Notes	Twin Pack	2.50	15	10	20
K238	Personal Organiser Files	Single	12.75	13	10	20
K276	Clear Plastic Pockets	100	8.50	15	15	30
K261	Box File	Single	3.75	28	15	40
K347	Lever Arch File	Single	1.95	32	15	40
L111	Clipboard	Single	2.50	27	20	35
K284	A4 Ring Binders	10	13.00	9	10	40
K236	Expanding File	Single	6.70	10	15	15
P211	Cash Box Size 1	Single	12.50	6	5	5
NEW RECORDS - 5						
P475	Key Cabinet - 40 keys	Single	39.99	4	3	5
P476	Key Cabinet - 60 keys	Single	46.25	1	3	5
NEW RECORDS - 10						
P212	Cash Box - Size 2	Single	14.00	8	5	5
P213	Cash Box - Size 3	Single	16.50	6	5	5

9 The suspension files, K299, are no longer available, delete the stock record.

10 Add the two new stock items as shown on Data Sheet 1 – NEW RECORDS – 10.

11 The following items of stock have been received, so add them to the relevant stock records:

REFERENCE	NUMBER	REFERENCE	NUMBER
T275	100	K236	15
E196	45	P476	5
K284	40		

12 Print the revised stock list.

13 The following items of stock have been sold so delete from the stock levels:

REFERENCE	NUMBER
E186	4
M101	2
K238	2

?

DO YOU KNOW?

How to print a list of items which do *not* need reordering?

14 Print two summary reports showing:

(a) items which need reordering
(b) items which do *not* need ordering.

15 Print a summary showing the total cost of ordering these items which are low on stock.

?

DO YOU KNOW?

How to get a directory listing?

How to print a directory listing?

TASK 2

1 Log on to the system.

2 Obtain a directory listing of your work disk (or user area) and print one copy.

3 Load the stock control program.

4 Enter the data for the stock items shown on DATA SHEET 2.

?

DO YOU KNOW?

How to make a back-up copy of a file?

5 Save the file and make a back-up copy.

6 Print a complete stock list.

7 Print a report showing:

(a) the items which are understocked
(b) the cost of ordering the understocked items.

8 Add the two new stock items listed on Data Sheet 2 – NEW RECORDS – 8.

9 The following items have been received, so amend the individual records:

REFERENCE	NUMBER	REFERENCE	NUMBER
8231	50	8282	50
8246	25	8257	20

10 Items 8243 and 8202 are no longer available and should be deleted from the stock list.

11 Item 8255 has not been selling well and the price is to be reduced by £1.50.

12 Add the two new stock items as shown on Data Sheet 2 – NEW RECORDS – 12.

13 Following a sales drive, the following items have been sold and need to be deleted from the records:

REFERENCE	NUMBER	REFERENCE	NUMBER
8215	10	8180	25
8251	5	8142	9
8260	4	8270	3
8267	3		

14 Print a complete stock list.

DATA SHEET 2 – STOCK CONTROL

REF	DESCRIPTION	UNIT	VALUE £	STOCK LEVEL	MINIMUM LEVEL	REORDER QUANTITY
8279	Folk and Fairisle Patterns	Single	3.95	105	50	100
8231	Card 1 Book	Single	4.25	19	30	50
8243	Card 3 Book	Single	4.75	36	30	50
8255	Long Cleaning Brush	Single	2.95	41	25	25
8246	Cleaning Fluid	2 litres	5.99	16	20	25
8202	Easy View Magnifier	Single	12.20	14	10	20
8215	Radiator Airer	Threes	5.25	21	15	15
8294	Needles	Pack of 10	2.90	75	50	100
8251	Colour Changer	Single	119.95	6	5	5
8282	Blank Design Cards 1	Pack of 50	4.75	35	40	50
8260	Card Punch	Single	11.95	13	10	10
8267	Tension Arm	Single	15.95	7	5	5
8257	Ribber Cover	Single	5.25	17	20	20
8269	Tuition Video - Beginners	Single	9.99	18	15	15
8033	Floral Cuffs	Pair	1.25	74	50	50
NEW RECORDS - 8						
8180	Wool Winder	Single	12.95	98	50	100
8142	Wool Box	Set	5.45	38	25	50
NEW RECORDS - 12						
8049	Blank Design Cards 2	Pack of 50	4.75	40	40	30
8270	Tuition Video - Intermediate	Single	9.99	21	15	15

15 Print two reports showing:

(a) the items which need restocking
(b) the cost of replacing the understocked items.

16 Delete the file.

17 Print a copy of the directory to prove that the file has been deleted.

TASK 3

1 Log on to the system.

2 Load the stock control program.

3 Enter the data for the stock items shown on Data Sheet 3.

4 Print a complete stock list.

5 Print two reports showing:

(a) the items which are understocked
(b) the cost of ordering the items which are understocked.

6 Change the price of items 104 and 141 to £1.55.

7 Add the two new stock items shown on Data Sheet 3 – NEW RECORDS – 7.

8 Items 175 and 178 are no longer stocked. Delete the records accordingly.

9 All understocked items have been reordered and received. Amend the relevant stock level records by adding the reorder quantity.

10 Print a complete stock list.

11 Items 159 and 167 are no longer stocked. Delete the records accordingly.

12 Add the two new stock items shown on Data Sheet 3 – NEW RECORDS – 12.

13 The following items have been sold, so remove them from the stock level:

REFERENCE	NUMBER	REFERENCE	NUMBER
163	5	182	7
104	8	149	5
141	5		

DATA SHEET 3 – STOCK CONTROL

REF	DESCRIPTION	UNIT	VALUE £	STOCK LEVEL	MINIMUM LEVEL	REORDER QUANTITY
191	Tie Wrap	100	2.10	32	40	50
182	Battery Charger Clips	10	1.90	49	25	50
175	Test Lead Kit	Single	1.98	8	10	10
163	15-way Latching Mechanism	Single	.52	24	20	20
178	26-way Printer Cable	Single	7.95	29	20	25
167	2-pin Chassis Socket	10	1.35	63	50	50
159	3-pin Chassis Socket	10	1.80	69	50	50
167	Screened Plug	Single	.68	17	20	25
121	Plastic Barrel Plug	Single	.55	62	50	100
136	T Adaptor	Single	1.98	24	25	25
187	Lined Socket	Single	.28	42	30	40
195	Mini-headphone Splitter	Single	1.95	3	5	15
182	Two into One Adaptor	Single	.88	15	10	20
123	Cassette Mains Lead	Single	.68	7	10	10
104	Four pole Connector	Single	1.95	31	25	25
NEW RECORDS - 7						
141	Six pole Connector	Single	1.35	40	25	25
149	Insulating Boot	Single	.28	24	20	30
NEW RECORDS - 12						
127	8 Pin Video Plug	Single	2.80	30	15	25
175	Video Lead	Single	1.98	36	20	20

14 Print a complete stock list.

15 Print two reports showing:

(a) the items which are understocked
(b) the cost of replacing the items which are understocked.

?

DO YOU KNOW?
How to format a disk?
How to delete individual documents from a disk?
How to make a back-up copy of your disk?

TASK 4

1 List the directory of your disk on the screen and print one copy.

2 Delete any documents you no longer require.

3 Format a new disk for use later.

4 Load the stock control program.

5 Enter the data for stock records as shown on Data Sheet 4.

6 Print the following:

(a) a complete stock list
(b) the understocked items
(c) the cost of ordering the understocked items.

7 Insert the new stock items as shown on Data Sheet 4 – NEW RECORDS – 7.

8 Increase the prices of all G-referenced items by £1.

9 Delete G519 and F803, which are no longer stocked.

10 Insert the new stock items as shown on Data Sheet 4 – NEW RECORDS – 10.

11 H500 and F937 are not selling and they have been removed from stock. Delete the records accordingly.

DATA SHEET 4 – STOCK CONTROL

REF	DESCRIPTION	UNIT	VALUE £	STOCK LEVEL	MINIMUM LEVEL	REORDER QUANTITY
G217	Air Compressor	Single	17.99	7	10	15
H500	Travel Rug	Single	4.99	12	10	10
F222	Car Vac	Single	14.95	36	20	20
H479	Warning Triangle	Single	6.99	39	20	30
H322	Car Carpet	Set	6.99	42	30	35
H723	Fire Extinguisher	Single	9.99	10	15	30
G361	Timing Light	Single	19.49	8	10	10
G700	Axle Stands	Pair	18.99	7	5	10
G519	Two Ton Bottle Jack	Single	7.99	13	10	10
G266	Electronic Alarm	Single	18.49	17	20	25
F100	Smoke Alarm	Single	17.99	12	20	30
F937	Kitchen Fire Blanket	Single	11.99	14	10	10
F803	Home Safety Kit	Single	44.95	9	5	10
F264	PBD Plug	Single	17.99	3	5	10
G500	PBD Two Adaptor	Single	15.99	12	5	10
NEW RECORDS - 7						
J100	PBD Twin Socket	Single	35.99	11	5	10
J327	PBD Single Socket	Single	18.99	9	5	10
NEW RECORDS - 10						
J519	Security File	Single	57.99	3	3	2
K200	Welcome Light	Single	49.95	8	5	10

12 Amend the stock levels for the following items which have been sold:

REFERENCE	NUMBER	REFERENCE	NUMBER
G700	3	F100	5
F222	4	G500	5
K200	4		

13 Print a complete stock list.

14 Print two reports showing:

(a) a list of understocked items
(b) the price of understocked items.

15 All the items which were understocked have now been purchased. Amend the stock level by adding the reorder quantity.

16 Print a complete stock list.

17 Using the newly formatted disk, make a copy of the files created in this Task.

TASK 5

1 Load the stock control program.

2 Enter the data for the stock records shown on Data Sheet 5.

3 Print a complete stock list.

4 Add the new stock items given on Data Sheet 5 – NEW RECORDS – 4.

5 Print two reports showing:

(a) understocked items
(b) cost of purchasing understocked items.

6 Items R37 and A12 are to be deleted from the records.

7 The understocked items have now been reordered and received. Amend the stock levels by adding the reorder quantity to the stock level.

DATA SHEET 5 – STOCK CONTROL

REF	DESCRIPTION	UNIT	VALUE £	STOCK LEVEL	MINIMUM LEVEL	REORDER QUANTITY
T31	Speaker Stands	Pair	16.95	8	10	10
A12	72 Cassette Cabinet	Single	12.75	46	25	30
C9	Compact Disk Cabinet	Single	9.95	23	25	30
A16	Cassette Cleaning Kit	Single	4.95	52	50	75
C12	CD Cleaning Kit	Single	4.95	43	40	60
R37	Record Cleaning Kit	Single	4.95	27	25	75
V10	Video Cassette Library Case	Pack of 4	8.95	65	50	50
V15	Video Tape E180	Twin Pack	7.95	79	100	250
V16	Video Tape E180	Pack of 3	9.95	71	75	200
V17	Video Tape E240	Single	4.15	89	100	250
V18	Video Tape E240	Twin Pack	8.95	65	100	200
V19	Video Connecting Leads	Single	9.95	29	25	25
T10	Scart Connector	Single	17.95	7	10	15
A19	Stereo Headphones	Single	9.95	42	30	30
A49	C90 Audio Cassettes	Pack of 5	4.95	60	75	125
NEW RECORDS - 4						
A56	Personal Stereo Headphones	Single	16.95	30	20	20
T11	Set Top Aerial	Single	6.45	15	10	15
NEW RECORDS - 11						
T15	TV Aerial Extension Lead	Single	3.75	18	10	20
V20	Video Head Cleaner	Single	5.95	41	30	50

8 The following items have been sold, so amend by changing the stock level:

REFERENCE	NUMBER	REFERENCE	NUMBER
A16	14	T11	8
C12	5	T31	8
A56	19	V19	7

9 Decrease the price of A16 by 50p.

10 Increase the price of V10 by 50p.

11 Add the two new stock items given on Data Sheet 5 – NEW RECORDS – 11.

12 Print a complete stock list.

13 Print two reports showing:

(a) the items which are understocked
(b) the cost of purchasing the items which are understocked.

Assignment 1—Stock control

Section 1 – Objectives 040, 041, 042, 043, 044, 045*

Section 2 – Objectives 056, 057, 058, 059, 060, 061, 062, 063, 064, 065, 070

1 Format a blank disk (*or* select an empty user area).

2 Start up the system and load the stock control program.

3 Enter the data for the stock items as given on Assignment Data Sheet 1.

4 List the directory of files and save your stock file using an appropriate file name.

5 Load the printer with paper. Set to top of form. Print a full stock list.

6 Make a back-up copy of your file on to the newly formatted disk (*or* copy the file to the newly selected user area.

7 Reload your original file.

8 Add the two new stock items to the file given on Assignment Data Sheet 1.

9 Increase the price of S217 and T277 by 25p.

10 As stock item T246 is no longer available, delete this stock record.

11 Print out two summary reports showing:

(a) items which need reordering
(b) items which do *not* need reordering.

12 Print out the total cost of reordering all items below minimum reorder level.

13 Save your amended file.

14 Delete your back-up file.

15 Close down the system.

ASSIGNMENT 1 – DATA SHEET

REF	DESCRIPTION	UNIT	VALUE £	STOCK LEVEL	MINIMUM LEVEL	REORDER QUANTITY
P176	Triple Mirror	Single	33.95	8	5	10
P322	Hat and Coat Stand	Single	13.95	12	10	15
T139	Hall Table	Single	22.95	4	5	5
R198	Stainless Steel Cutlery	24 piece	16.50	18	15	15
S521	Stainless Steel Cutlery	44 piece	22.50	14	10	15
T781	White Wine Glasses	6	4.99	72	50	50
R222	Red Wine Glasses	6	4.50	64	50	50
P555	Fruit Set	7 piece	13.99	81	40	50
T111	Brandy Glasses	2	10.99	39	50	50
S217	Whisky Glasses	4	16.50	45	50	50
S844	Champagne Glasses	4	16.99	33	50	50
T277	Casserole Set	3 piece	12.50	24	50	100
P558	Steak Plates	6	11.50	16	25	40
P101	Napkin Rings	6	10.99	92	60	100
T246	Knife Set and Rack	4 piece	27.50	19	15	15
NEW RECORDS - 8						
V874	Microwave Cook Set	9 piece	17.50	32	20	20
W283	Chinese Wok	Single	15.75	17	10	15

Assignment 2—Stock control

Section 1 – Objectives 040, 041, 042, 043, 044, 045*

Section 2 – Objectives 056, 057, 058, 059, 060, 061, 062, 063, 064, 065, 070

1 Format a blank disk (*or* select an empty user area).

2 Start up the system and load the stock control program.

3 List the directory and select a suitable file name.

4 Enter the data for the stock items as given on Assignment 2 Data Sheet.

5 Save the stock file.

6 Load the printer with paper. Set to top of form. Print a full stock list.

7 Make a back-up copy of your file onto the newly formatted disk *or* copy the file to the user area. Reload the original file.

8 Add the two new stock items to the file as given on Assignment 2 Data Sheet.

9 The ankle and wrist weights are no longer being stocked. Delete the record from the file.

10 Increase the price of item 4449 by 50p.

Decrease the price of item 4333 by £5.00.

11 Print out two summary reports showing:

(a) items which need reordering
(b) items which do not need reordering.

12 Print out the total cost of reordering all items below minimum reorder level.

13 Save your amended file.

14 Delete your back-up file.

15 Close down the system.

ASSIGNMENT 2 – DATA SHEET

REF	DESCRIPTION	UNIT	VALUE £	STOCK LEVEL	MINIMUM LEVEL	REORDER QUANTITY
4217	Rowing Machine	Single	42.99	7	5	5
4386	Exercise Wheel	Single	4.99	8	10	15
4266	Exercise Mat	Single	12.99	19	20	20
4350	Ankle/Wrist Weights	Single	7.99	26	20	15
4449	Ladies Midi Sports Bag	Single	9.99	42	30	50
4452	Exercise Bench	Single	39.99	7	5	5
4837	Family Weight Set	Set	16.99	21	15	20
4242	26 kilo Dumbbell Set	Set	14.99	15	12	8
4999	Barbell/Dumbbell Set	Set	9.99	34	25	50
4101	Rower	Single	47.99	4	3	3
4662	Sit-up Bar	Single	4.99	7	10	20
4789	Punchbag Mitts	Pair	9.99	15	20	20
4333	Speedball Set	Set	39.99	3	5	5
4111	Punch Bag	Single	14.99	13	10	10
4222	Crunchboard	Single	14.99	9	5	5
4921	Abdominal Board	Single	19.99	3	10	15
4987	Stowaway Rower	Single	64.99	2	3	5

NEW RECORDS - 8

4321	Floor to Ceiling Punchbag	Single	22.50	16	10	15
4123	Cambered Bar	Single	8.99	32	20	20

7 Payroll

DO YOU KNOW?

What *Income Tax* is?

What *National Insurance* is?

What a *tax code* is?

How *gross* pay is arrived at?

How *net* pay is arrived at?

What *statutory* deductions are?

What *voluntary* deductions are?

TASK 1

1. Start up the system.
2. Format a blank disk.
3. Load a payroll program.

DO YOU KNOW?

How to enter employee records?

How to enter the hours worked in a week?

How to print a payroll list?

How to print individual payslips?

4. Enter the records for the following four employees?

```
Emp No 222     Joseph Alexander
Emp No 223     Philip Morris
Emp No 224     Alison Tate
Emp No 225     Jane Gould
```

Note:

(1) All employees are NHI Status A.

(2) Employee's and Employer's NI contributions are always the same.

EMP NO	HOURLY RATE OF PAY	TAX CODE	GROSS PAY TO DATE	TOTAL TAX TO DATE	O/TIME RATE	NI TO DATE
222	2.40	315L	96.00	8.75	3.20	6.72
223	2.10	242L	84.00	9.25	2.80	5.88
224	2.70	210L	108.00	16.75	3.60	7.56
225	2.85	210L	114.00	18.25	3.80	7.98

5. Enter the hours shown on the time sheet for Week 2.

TIME SHEET FOR WEEK 2

NAME	NORMAL HOURS	O/TIME HOURS
Joseph Alexander	40	3
Philip Morris	40	2
Alison Tate	40	-
Jane Gould	40	1

6 Print a payroll list.

7 Print a payslip for each employee.

?

DO YOU KNOW?
How to make amendments to employee records?
How to add employee records?
How to delete employee records?

8 Alison Tate has married. Her name is now Alison Prescot.

9 Frank Edward Childs (Emp No 226) joined the firm on 13th April. Add a new record for him.

EMP NO	HOURLY RATE OF PAY	TAX CODE	GROSS PAY TO DATE	TOTAL TAX TO DATE	O/TIME RATE	NI TO DATE
226	2.40	239L	192.00	24.75	3.20	13.44

10 Enter the hours shown on the time sheet for Week 3.

TIME SHEET FOR WEEK 3

NAME	NORMAL HOURS	O/TIME HOURS
Joseph Alexander	40	4
Philip Morris	40	3
Alison Prescot	40	1
Jane Gould	40	-
Frank E Childs	40	-

11 Print a payroll list.

12 The following have joined the firm. Add their records to the file.

Emp No 228	Gillian Done
Emp No 227	Terence Donnelley

EMP NO	HOURLY RATE OF PAY	TAX CODE	GROSS PAY TO DATE	TOTAL TAX TO DATE	O/TIME RATE	NI TO DATE
227	3.00	210L	360.00	59.50	4.00	32.40
228	2.10	345H	252.00	13.00	2.80	17.64

13 Joseph Alexander and Jane Gould have left the firm. Delete them from the records.

14 Philip Morris has had a tax code change from 242L to 252L.

15 Search for all employees with tax codes of 210L and change them to 220L.

16 The hourly rate for Terence Donnelley has changed to £3.30.

17 Enter the hours shown on the time sheet for Week 4.

TIME SHEET FOR WEEK 4

NAME	NORMAL HOURS	O/TIME HOURS
Terence Donnelley	40	2
Philip Morris	40	3
Alison Prescot	40	2
Frank E Childs	40	1
Gillian Done	40	3

18 Print a payroll list.

19 Hilary Evans (Emp No 229) has joined the firm. She has not worked before.

EMP NO	HOURLY RATE OF PAY	TAX CODE	GROSS PAY TO DATE	TOTAL TAX TO DATE	O/TIME RATE	NI TO DATE
229	3.00	276L			4.00	

20 The name printed on the payslip for Terence Donnelley is incorrect, it should read Terence Donnelly. Make the necessary amendment.

21 Change all tax codes by adding 10 points.

22 There have been some changes in pay rates as follows:

Gillian Done – hourly rate increased to £2.40
Frank Childs – hourly rate increased to £2.70
Alison Prescot – now works 35 and not 40 hours per week.

23 Search the payroll for all those employees who are earning more than £80 per week.

24 Enter the hours shown on the time sheet for Week 5.

TIME SHEET FOR WEEK 5

NAME	NORMAL HOURS	O/TIME HOURS
Philip Morris	40	1
Alison Prescot	35	-
Frank E Childs	40	1
Terence Donnelly	40	-
Gillian Done	40	2
Hilary Evans	40	-

25 Print a payroll list.

26 Print payslips for each employee.

27 Save the records and make a back-up copy.

28 Close down the system.

TASK 2

1 Start up the system.

2 Format a blank disk *or* select an empty user area.

3 Load a payroll program.

4 Enter the records for the following four employees:

Emp No 210	Phillipa Kinsella
Emp No 211	John Frederick Thompson
Emp No 212	Elizabeth Laura Rimmer
Emp No 213	Richard Paul Lindley

Note:

(1) All employees are NHI Status A.

(2) Employee's and employer's NI contributions are always the same.

EMP NO	HOURLY RATE OF PAY	TAX CODE	GROSS PAY TO DATE	TOTAL TAX TO DATE	O/TIME RATE	NI TO DATE
210	3.00	210L	105.00	16.00	4.00	7.35
211	1.80	257L	63.00	3.25	2.40	3.15
212	2.10	210L	73.50	8.00	2.80	3.67
213	2.10	316L	73.50	3.00	2.80	3.67

5 Enter the hours worked in Week 2 from the timesheet below:

6 Print a complete payroll list.

7 Print payslips for each employee.

TIME SHEET FOR WEEK 2

NAME	NORMAL HOURS	O/TIME HOURS
Phillipa Kinsella	35	2
John F Thompson	35	2
Elizabeth L Rimmer	35	3
Richard P Lindley	35	4

8 A new employee, Melissa Southern (Emp No 214) has joined the company.

EMP NO	HOURLY RATE OF PAY	TAX CODE	GROSS PAY TO DATE	TOTAL TAX TO DATE	O/TIME RATE	NI TO DATE
214	2.40	210L	168.00	21.50	3.20	11.76

9 Change the tax code for J F Thompson to 210L.

10 Enter the hours worked in Week 3 from the time sheet below:

TIME SHEET FOR WEEK 3

NAME	NORMAL HOURS	O/TIME HOURS
Phillipa Kinsella	35	1
John F Thompson	35	1
Elizabeth Rimmer	35	2
Richard P Lindley	35	1
Melissa Southern	35	-

11 Print a complete payroll list.

12 Add a new employee, Lionel F C Copeland (Emp No 215) to the payroll.

EMP NO	HOURLY RATE OF PAY	TAX CODE	GROSS PAY TO DATE	TOTAL TAX TO DATE	O/TIME RATE	NI TO DATE
215	2.70	296L	283.50	28.00	3.60	11.83

13 Phillipa Kinsella has left the firm. Delete her details from the payroll records.

14 Elizabeth Rimmer has married. Her married name is Broxton. Make the necessary amendments to the records.

15 Search for all employees with net pay of less than £70 per week.

16 Melissa Southern has had her hourly rate changed to £2.70.

17 Insert the hours worked in Week 4 from the time sheet below:

TIME SHEET FOR WEEK 4

NAME	NORMAL HOURS	O/TIME HOURS
John F Thompson	35	2
Elizabeth Broxton	35	2
Richard Lindley	35	1
Melissa Southern	35	3
Lionel F C Copeland	35	2

18 Print a complete payroll list.

19 Make the following changes to the records:

The hourly rate for Elizabeth Broxton has changed to £2.40
Richard Lindley now works 40 hour a week
Change all tax codes by adding 10 points.

20 Enter the hours worked in Week 5 from the time sheet below:

TIME SHEET FOR WEEK 5

NAME	NORMAL HOURS	O/TIME HOURS
John F Thompson	35	1
Elizabeth Broxton	35	-
Richard Lindley	40	2
Melissa Southern	35	-
Lionel F C Copeland	35	1

21 Print a complete payroll list.

22 Print a payslip for each employee.

23 Save and back-up the data for the final week.

24 Close down the system.

TASK 3

1 Start up the system.

2 Format a blank disk.

3 Load a payroll program.

4 Enter the records for the following four employees:

Emp No 216	James Dixon
Emp No 217	Doris Vera Palin
Emp No 218	Annette Cunningham
Emp No 219	Brenda Atherton

Note:

(1) All employees are NHI Status A.

(2) Employee's and employer's NI contributions are always the same.

EMP NO	HOURLY RATE OF PAY	TAX CODE	GROSS PAY TO DATE	TOTAL TAX TO DATE	O/TIME RATE	NI TO DATE
216	2.70	240L	94.50	12.00	3.60	6.61
217	2.40	210L	84.00	10.75	3.20	5.88
218	2.10	210L	73.50	8.00	2.80	3.67
219	2.10	215L	73.50	7.75	2.80	3.67

5 Enter the hours worked in Week 2 from the time sheet below:

TIME SHEET FOR WEEK 2

NAME	NORMAL HOURS	O/TIME HOURS
Annette Cunningham	35	2
Brenda Atherton	35	1
James Dixon	35	-
Doris Vera Palin	35	3

6 Print a complete payroll list.

7 Print a payslip for each employee.

8 Annette Cunningham has married and her name should be changed to Annette Johnson.

9 The tax code for James Dixon should be changed to 250L.

10 Kenneth Andrews (Emp No 220) joined the company on 12th April. Add his record to the file.

EMP NO	HOURLY RATE OF PAY	TAX CODE	GROSS PAY TO DATE	TOTAL TAX TO DATE	O/TIME RATE	NI TO DATE
220	3.00	220L	210.00	31.25	4.00	14.70

11 Enter the hours worked in Week 3 from the time sheet below:

TIME SHEET FOR WEEK 3

NAME	NORMAL HOURS	O/TIME HOURS
Annette Johnson	35	1
Brenda Atherton	35	-
James Dixon	35	2
Doris Palin	35	1
Kenneth Andrews	35	3

12 Print a complete payroll list.

13 A new employee, Mark Phillipsen (Emp No 221), has joined the company. Add his record to the file.

EMP NO	HOURLY RATE OF PAY	TAX CODE	GROSS PAY TO DATE	TOTAL TAX TO DATE	O/TIME RATE	NI TO DATE
221	2.70	235L	283.50	36.75	3.60	19.83

14 Annette Johnson has left the company. Delete her record from the file.

15 Doris Palin's tax code has changed to 220L.

16 Brenda Atherton has married. Her new name is Saunderson.

17 Search for all employees with a tax code of 210L.

18 Enter the hours worked in Week 4 from the time sheet below:

TIME SHEET FOR WEEK 4

NAME	NORMAL HOURS	O/TIME HOURS
Brenda Saunderson	35	3
James Dixon	35	2
Doris Palin	35	3
Kenneth Andrews	35	2
Mark Phillipsen	35	-

19 Print a complete payroll list.

20 Make the following changes to the payroll records:

Mark Philipson has reported that his name has been spelt incorrectly. Change from Phillipsen to Philipson.
Change all tax codes by adding 10 points.
Change the hourly rate of Mrs Palin to £2.70.
Brenda Sanderson has reported that her name has been spelt incorrectly. Change from Saunderson to Sanderson.

21 Enter the hours worked in Week 5 from the time sheet below:

TIME SHEET FOR WEEK 5

NAME	NORMAL HOURS	O/TIME HOURS
Brenda Sanderson	35	1
James Dixon	35	2
Doris Palin	35	1
Kenneth Andrews	35	2
Mark Philipson	35	-

22 Print a complete payroll list.

23 Print a payslip for each employee.

24 Save and back-up the file.

25 Connect your computer to another source and send the following message:

CLAIT Payroll Exercises

I have completed three payroll exercises, and I am becoming quite proficient in the use of the payroll package.

Signed:

Date:

26 Close down the system.

TASK 4

1 Start up the system.

2 Format a blank disk *or* select an empty user area.

3 Load a payroll program.

Remember to back-up the data when told to do so by your program. If you are not told – back up after each week has been completed.

4 Enter the details for the following four employees:

Emp No 422	Ernest Anstey
Emp No 423	Joseph Hatfield
Emp No 424	Helen Jane Crosbie
Emp No 425	Graham Conway

EMP NO	HOURLY RATE OF PAY	TAX CODE	GROSS PAY TO DATE	TOTAL TAX TO DATE	O/TIME RATE	NI TO DATE
422	2.40	270L	91.20	9.75	3.20	6.38
423	2.70	225L	102.60	14.75	3.60	7.18
424	2.10	295L	79.80	5.50	2.80	5.59
425	2.70	255L	102.60	13.25	3.60	7.18

5 Enter the hours worked in Week 2 as given in the time sheet below:

TIME SHEET FOR WEEK 2

NAME	NORMAL HOURS	O/TIME HOURS
Ernest Anstey	38	1
Joseph Hatfield	38	2
Helen Jane Crosbie	38	2
Graham Conway	38	1

6 Print a complete payroll list.

7 Print a payslip for each employee.

8 Helen Jane Crosbie's name has been spelt incorrectly. It should be Crosby, so change the record accordingly.

9 Change the tax code for Ernest Anstey from 270L to 280L.

10 A new employee, Phyllis Foster (Emp No 426), has joined the company. Set up the necessary records.

EMP NO	HOURLY RATE OF PAY	TAX CODE	GROSS PAY TO DATE	TOTAL TAX TO DATE	O/TIME RATE	NI TO DATE
426	1.80	222L	136.80	12.75	2.40	6.84

11 Enter the hours worked in Week 3 as given in the time sheet below:

TIME SHEET FOR WEEK 3

NAME	NORMAL HOURS	O/TIME HOURS
Ernest Anstey	38	2
Joseph Hatfield	38	2
Helen Crosby	38	1
Graham Conway	38	2
Phyllis Foster	38	3

12 Print a complete payroll list.

13 A new employee, Freda Hammond (Emp No 427) has joined the company. Set up the necessary records.

EMP NO	HOURLY RATE OF PAY	TAX CODE	GROSS PAY TO DATE	TOTAL TAX TO DATE	O/TIME RATE	NI TO DATE
427	1.80	216L	205.20	20.00	2.40	10.26

14 Ernest Anstey and Graham Conway have both left the company. Delete their records from the file.

15 Phyllis Foster has married. Her name is now Phyllis Andersen and her tax code has changed to 210L.

16 Enter the hours worked in Week 4 as given in the time sheet below:

TIME SHEET FOR WEEK 4

NAME	NORMAL HOURS	O/TIME HOURS
Joseph Hatfield	38	1
Helen Crosby	38	1
Freda Hammond	38	1
Phyllis Andersen	38	2

17 Print a complete payroll list.

18 Phyllis Anderson has reported that her name has been spelt incorrectly. It should be Anderson and not Andersen. Her rate of pay has changed to £2.40 and her overtime rate to £3.20.

19 Helen Crosby has had a tax code change. It should be 275L.

20 Enter the hours worked in Week 5 as given in the time sheet below:

TIME SHEET FOR WEEK 5

NAME	NORMAL HOURS	O/TIME HOURS
Joseph Hatfield	38	2
Helen Crosby	38	2
Freda Hammond	38	2
Phyllis Anderson	38	2

21 Print a complete payroll list.

22 Print a payslip for each employee.

23 Save and back-up the data file.

24 Close down the system.

TASK 5

1 Start up the system.

2 Format a blank disk *or* select an empty user area.

3 Load a payroll program.

Remember to back-up the data when told to do so by your program. If you are not told – back-up after each week has been completed.

4 Enter the details for the following four employees:

Emp No 502	Philip Moore
Emp No 503	Alison Sydney
Emp No 504	Dennis Smythson
Emp No 505	Karen Johnson

EMP NO	HOURLY RATE OF PAY	TAX CODE	GROSS PAY TO DATE	TOTAL TAX TO DATE	O/TIME RATE	NI TO DATE
502	2.10	275L	73.50	5.00	2.80	3.67
503	2.40	210L	84.00	10.75	3.20	5.88
504	3.00	240L	105.00	14.50	4.00	7.35
505	1.80	210L	84.00	10.75	3.20	5.88

5 Enter the hours worked in Week 2 as given in the time sheet below:

TIME SHEET FOR WEEK 2

NAME	NORMAL HOURS	O/TIME HOURS
Philip Moore	35	3
Alison Sydney	35	2
Dennis Smythson	35	2
Karen Johnson	35	1

6 Print a payroll list.

7 Print a payslip for each employee.

8 Make the following changes to the records:

Alison Sydney is now married. Her new name is Alison Trent.
Philip Moore has had a tax code change to 255L.
The hourly rate for Karen Johnson has been increased to £2.10 and her overtime rate to £2.80.

9 Dennis Smythson has left the company. Delete the appropriate records from the file.

10 A new employee, Mark Peterson (Emp No 506), has joined the company. Set up the appropriate records. He has never worked before.

EMP NO	HOURLY RATE OF PAY	TAX CODE	GROSS PAY TO DATE	TOTAL TAX TO DATE	O/TIME RATE	NI TO DATE
506	2.70	250L			3.60	

11 Enter the hours worked in Week 3 as given in the time sheet below:

TIME SHEET FOR WEEK 3

NAME	NORMAL HOURS	O/TIME HOURS
Philip Moore	35	3
Alison Trent	35	1
Mark Peterson	35	-
Karen Johnson	35	1

12 Print a complete payroll list.

13 Make the following changes to the records:

Karen Johnson has married and is now known as Karen Carter.
Alison Trent has had a tax code change to 220L.

14 Philip Moore has left the company. Delete the appropriate records.

15 A new employee, Regina Prince (Emp No 507) has joined the company. Set up the appropriate records. She has not worked before.

EMP NO	HOURLY RATE OF PAY	TAX CODE	GROSS PAY TO DATE	TOTAL TAX TO DATE	O/TIME RATE	NI TO DATE
507	2.40	210L			3.20	

16 Search for all employees earning £2.40 per hour.

17 Enter the hours worked in Week 4 as given in the time sheet below:

TIME SHEET FOR WEEK 4

NAME	NORMAL HOURS	O/TIME HOURS
Regina Prince	35	2
Alison Trent	35	2
Mark Peterson	35	3
Karen Carter	35	2

18 Print the complete payroll list.

19 Print a payslip for each employee.

20 Save and back-up the data.

21 Connect your computer to another source and send the following message:

CLAIT Payroll Exercises

I have now completed all the payroll exercises and am ready to progress to the mock assignments.

Signed:

Date:

22 Close down the system.

Assignment 1—Payroll

Section 1 – Objectives 041, 042, 043, 044, 045*

Section 2 – Objectives 056, 057, 058, 059, 060, 061, 062, 063, 064, 065, 067, 070, 071

1 Format a blank disk *or* select an empty user area.

2 Start up the system and load the payroll program.

3 Enter the details of the four employees given below. Assume they have just joined the company, and have not worked in this financial year.

Emp No 272	Peter Frinton
Emp No 273	Helen Carter
Emp No 274	Terence Halliday
Emp No 275	Martin Maxwell

EMP NO	HOURLY RATE OF PAY	TAX CODE	GROSS PAY TO DATE	TOTAL TAX TO DATE	O/TIME RATE	NI TO DATE
272	2.10	300H			2.80	
273	2.40	210L			3.20	
274	2.40	250L			3.20	
275	2.70	300H			3.60	

Note: All employees are NHI Status A.

4 Enter the hours worked in Week 2 of this financial year as shown in the time sheet below:

TIME SHEET FOR WEEK 2

NAME	NORMAL HOURS	O/TIME HOURS
Peter Frinton	35	3
Helen Carter	35	2
Terence Halliday	35	2
Martin Maxwell	35	1

5 Load the printer with paper, set to top of form and print out a full pay list.

6 Make a back-up copy of the file on to the newly formatted disk (*or* copy the file to the newly selected user area).

7 Reload the original file.

8 Search for employees with a tax code of 300H and change to 310H.

9 Add the new employee, Andrea Collins (Emp No 276) as shown below:

EMP NO	HOURLY RATE OF PAY	TAX CODE	GROSS PAY TO DATE	TOTAL TAX TO DATE	O/TIME RATE	NI TO DATE
276	2.10	210L			2.80	

10 Helen Carter, Employee No 273, has left the company; delete her record from the payroll.

11 Enter the details from the time sheet for week 3:

TIME SHEET FOR WEEK 3

NAME	NORMAL HOURS	O/TIME HOURS
Peter Frinton	35	2
Andrea Collins	35	2
Terence Halliday	35	1
Martin Maxwell	35	3

12 Print a payroll list for Week 3.

13 Produce a payslip for each employee in Week 3.

14 Delete the back-up file.

15 Connect your computer to another source and send the following message:

CLAIT Payroll Assignments

I have now completed the first of the two mock payroll assignments. I hope I have passed.

Signed:

Date:

16 Close down the system.

Assignment 2—Payroll

Section 1 – Objectives 041, 042, 043, 044, 045*

Section 2 – Objectives 056, 057, 058, 059, 060, 061, 062, 063, 064, 065, 067, 070, 071

1 Format a blank disk *or* select an empty user area.

2 Start up the system and load the payroll program.

3 Enter the details of the four employees given below. Assume they have just joined the company.

Emp No 602	Godfrey Marsh
Emp No 603	Raymond Taylor
Emp No 604	David Kent
Emp No 605	Agnes Lawson

EMP NO	HOURLY RATE OF PAY	TAX CODE	GROSS PAY TO DATE	TOTAL TAX TO DATE	O/TIME RATE	NI TO DATE
602	2.50	275L	95.00	10.25	3.20	6.65
603	2.60	275L	98.80	11.25	3.25	6.92
604	2.25	210L	85.50	11.00	3.00	5.98
605	2.50	210L	95.00	13.50	3.25	6.65

Note:

(1) All employees are NHI Status A.

(2) Employee's and employer's NI contributions are always the same.

4 Enter the hours worked in Week 2 of this financial year from the time sheet below:

TIME SHEET FOR WEEK 2

NAME	NORMAL HOURS	O/TIME HOURS
Godfrey Marsh	38	1
Raymond Taylor	38	-
David Kent	38	2
Agnes Lawson	38	3

5 Load the printer with paper, set to top of form and print a complete payroll list.

6 Back-up the data on to the newly formatted disk or on to the empty user area.

7 Reload the original file.

8 Add the new employee, Mrs Geraldine Collins (Emp No 606). This is her first job. The details are given below:

EMP NO	HOURLY RATE OF PAY	TAX CODE	GROSS PAY TO DATE	TOTAL TAX TO DATE	O/TIME RATE	NI TO DATE
606	2.10	220L			2.90	

9 David Kent has left the company. Delete his record.

10 Search for employees with an hourly rate of £2.50. Change it to £2.55. The overtime rate remains the same.

11 Enter the details from the time sheet for Week 3:

TIME SHEET FOR WEEK 3

NAME	NORMAL HOURS	O/TIME HOURS
Godfrey Marsh	38	2
Raymond Taylor	38	2
Geraldine Collins	38	3
Agnes Lawson	38	1

12 Print a complete payroll list for Week 3.

13 Produce a payslip for each employee for Week 3.

14 Delete the back-up file.

15 Connect your computer to another source and send the following message:

CLAIT Payroll Assignments

I have now completed two mock Assignments. I hope I have passed.

Signed:

Date:

16 Close down the system.

8 Viewdata

The tasks in this Section consist of making up pages on your local Viewdata system. Each Task is preceded by specific instructions as to how the page is to be displayed. When each page has been constructed, save the page and print one copy. If you cannot print your display, ask your tutor what you need to do to prove you have set up the page correctly.

?

DO YOU KNOW?

How to set up a page ready for typing a display?

How to use one, two and three colours?

How to make characters 'flash' on and off the screen?

How to put in background filling?

How to make characters double-height?

How to insert blocks of graphics into the page?

How to save the page?

How to print the page?

TASK 1 Make up the following page in one colour of text. Display the page as attractively as possible.

```
CARTER'S GARAGE

CAR SALE

EARLY ARRIVAL WILL GUARANTEE
A BARGAIN

ALL NEXT WEEK
```

TASK 2 Make up the following page using two colours – use the colours imaginatively.

```
SECONDHAND BOOKS

CLEARANCE SALE

All books must go

CONWAY CENTRE

15th  -  17th September
9 am to 9 pm
```

TASK 3 The following page is to be produced in three colours and with background filling:

```
SECONDHAND BOOKS

CLEARANCE SALE

1st Editions
19th Century Travel
Genealogy
```

TASK 4 Demonstrate your ability in making lines of text 'flash' on the screen, as well as using three colours and background filling.

```
FIRST AID CLASSES

DON'T PANIC

All you need to know to help others

CLASSES START NEXT WEEK
```

TASK 5 Display the following page attractively. The words FREE GIFTS should be double-height. VISIT OUR NEW SHOWROOM should be in flashing characters. Apart from using three colours, the remainder of the display is up to you.

```
FREE GIFTS

WHEN YOU BUY FROM OUR NEW SHOP

Portable Videos
VHS Tapes
Clock Radios
Teddy Bears

VISIT OUR NEW SHOWROOM
```

TASK 6 Use three colours, the words PERSONAL LOANS in double height characters, the AMOUNTS OF MONEY to be flashing characters, use background filling and use some form of graphics to make a decorative border at the bottom of the page.

```
PERSONAL LOANS

£1,000  to  £50,000

Need a Low Cost Loan?

GIVE US A BUZZ  ! !

CALL IN AND SEE US  ! !

MASTER SECURITIES
```

TASK 7 Use background filling, three colours, flashing characters, double height characters and a graphics display at the top and bottom of the page. Use your imagination in setting out the display.

```
THE GARDEN CENTRE
Willow Brook Way
SANDALL

FOR ALL YOUR GARDENING NEEDS

Plants
Shrubs
Lawn Mowers
Greenhouses
```

TASK 8 Use three colours, ANDERSTOWN GOLF RANGE in double height characters, OPENING OFFERS in flashing characters, graphics display at the bottom of the display and background filling.

```
ANDERSTOWN GOLF RANGE

BLACKHEATH

OPENING OFFERS

Ladies' Starter Sets
Golf Club Bargains
Clothing
Putters
```

TASK 9 Use three colours, EXCLUSIVE CONSERVATORIES in double height characters, PRICE in flashing characters, graphics display at the top and bottom of the display and background filling.

```
EXCLUSIVE CONSERVATORIES

Polycarbonate Roof
UPVC
Double Glazing

PRICE Including Installation

ONLY £3,990  +  VAT

FULLY GUARANTEED  -  RING TODAY
```

Assignment 1—Viewdata

Section 1 – Objectives 030, 031, 032, 033, 034, 035*, 036,*, 037*, 038*, 039*

Section 2 – Objectives 056, 057, 058, 059, 060, 062, 063

PART 1

1 Key in the Viewdata pages for Assignment 1 – TOP CAMERAS – and log on to the system.

2 Answer the following questions:

(a) What is the price of the polarising filter?
(b) What is the cost of the Queen lens, size 60–200 mm?
(c) Which is the most expensive Mercury camera?

PART 2

3 Compose the page for the detail given below. Use at least three colours, including a background filling.

The heading TOP CAMERAS should be double height. The word ACCESSORIES should flash. Using graphics, place a decorative block between Catalogue and Accessories.

4 Print the page.

```
TOP CAMERAS

CATALOGUE
ACCESSORIES

Clip Lens Cap          £1.99
Cable Release 10"      £2.65
Camera Case            £5.99
Filter Pouch           £2.95

Press 0 for Main Menu
```

5 Save the page as Page 11 and route it back to Page 1.

6 On Page 1 add one other item:

(5) Accessories

7 Change the routing of Page 1, Option 5 so that the newly created page can be accessed.

8 Close down the system.

ASSIGNMENT 1 – CANDIDATES' WORK SHEET

What is the price of the polarising filter? ______________________

What is the cost of the Queen lens, size 60–200 mm? ______________________

Which is the most expensive Mercury camera? ______________________

ASSIGNMENT 1 – VIEWDATA PAGES

These pages must be keyed in prior to the assignment using the Tree Diagram shown at the end of the assignment.

PAGE 0

```
TOP CAMERAS
CATALOGUE

LOOK TO US FIRST
FOR YOUR NEW CAMERA



Press 0 to continue
```

PAGE 1

```
TOP CAMERAS
CATALOGUE

(1)  Tripods
(2)  Cameras
(3)  Filters
(4)  Lenses

Press 0 for Last Menu
```

PAGE 11

```
TOP CAMERAS
CATALOGUE

TRIPODS

Target Telegrip     £97.75
Monopod             £73.99
Baby                £57.99
Tripod Case         £10.95

Press 0 for Last Menu
```

PAGE 12

```
TOP CAMERAS
CATALOGUE

CAMERAS

(1)  Janus
(2)  Saturn
(3)  Mercury

Press a number or
0 for Last Menu
```

PAGE 13

```
TOP CAMERAS
CATALOGUE

FILTERS

9 cool colours        £12.50
9 warm colours        £12.50
3 colour correction £5.00
3 neutral density     £3.50
1 polarising filter £42.50
Press 0 for Last Menu
```

PAGE 14

```
TOP CAMERAS
CATALOGUE

LENSES

(1)  Prince
(2)  Queen


Press a number of
0 for Last Menu
```

PAGE 121

```
TOP CAMERAS
CATALOGUE

JANUS CAMERAS

RTS7                £110.00
ST8001              £175.00
KR5 Super           £95.00
FT-1                £50.00

Press 0 for Last Menu
```

PAGE 122

```
TOP CAMERAS
CATALOGUE

SATURN CAMERAS

ME Super                 £170.00
230 AF                   £100.00
XR-P                     £75.00
PRJ10                    £55.00

Press 0 for Last Menu
```

PAGE 123

TOP CAMERAS
CATALOGUE

MERCURY CAMERAS

7000T	£65.00
9000T	£95.00
11000T	£125.00
13000T	£155.00

Press 0 for Last Menu

PAGE 141

TOP CAMERAS
CATALOGUE

PRINCE LENSES

28-70 mm	£125.00
35-135 mm	£180.00
75-200 mm	£165.00
70-210 mm	£90.00

Press 0 for Last Menu

PAGE 142

TOP CAMERAS
CATALOGUE

QUEEN LENSES

28-80 mm	£160.00
60-200 mm	£99.00
75-300 mm	£190.00
70-210 mm	£110.00

Press 0 for Last Menu

TREE DIAGRAM – ASSIGNMENT 1 – VIEWDATA

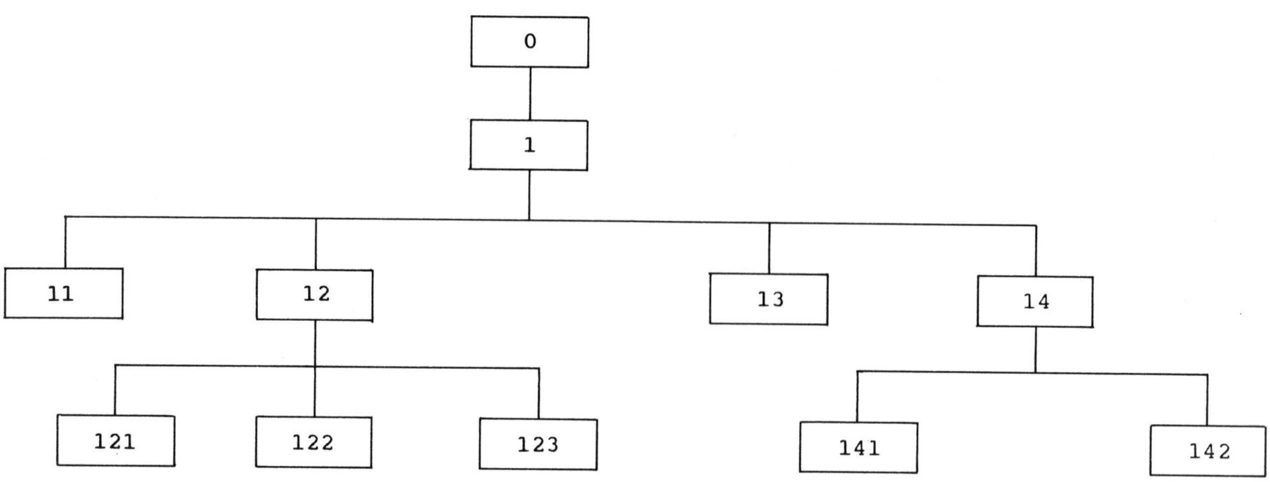

Assignment 2—Viewdata

Section 1 – Objectives 030, 031, 032, 033, 034, 035*, 036,*, 037*, 038*, 039*

Section 2 – Objectives 056, 057, 058, 059, 060, 062, 063

PART 1

1 Key in the Viewdata pages for Assignment 2 – CASTLES IN BRITAIN – and log on to the system.

2 Answer the following questions:

(a) What is the admission charge of Brugh Castle and when is it open?
(b) What is the telephone number for further details of castles in Ireland?
(c) Where is there an exhibition of paintings?

PART 2

3 Compose the page from the information given below. Use at least three colours, including a background filling.

The heading CASTLES IN EUROPE should be double-height. The phone number should flash. Use graphics to place a decorative block either side of the phone number.

```
CASTLES IN EUROPE

If you have a desire to
see the beautiful castles
which are open to visitors
in Europe

PHONE:  CastleEurope on
        51065789

Press 0 for Main Menu
```

4 Print the page.

5 Save the page as Page 2 and route it back to Page 0.

6 On Page 0 add the following items:

(1) Castles in Britain
(2) Castles in Europe

7 Change the routing of Page 0 so that the newly created page can be accessed.

8 Close down the system.

ASSIGNMENT 2 – CANDIDATES' WORK SHEET

1 What is the admission charge of Brugh Castle?

2 When is it open?

3 What is the telephone number for further details of castles in Ireland?

4 Where is there an exhibition of paintings?

ASSIGNMENT 2 – VIEWDATA PAGES

These pages must be keyed in prior to the assignment using the Tree Diagram shown at the end of the assignment.

PAGE 0

```
CASTLES

IN THE AIR

COME AND SEE US ! !

Press 0 to Continue
```

PAGE 1

```
MAIN INDEX

CASTLES IN BRITAIN

1    England
2    Ireland
3    Scotland
4    Wales

Press 0 to Continue
```

PAGE 11

```
CASTLES IN BRITAIN

ENGLAND

11    Stanton Castle
12    Brugh Castle
13    Ricardo Castle
14    Blair House

Press 0 for Main Menu or
a number to continue
```

PAGE 12

```
CASTLES IN BRITAIN

IRELAND

There are many beautiful
castles and houses in
Ireland.

Phone for details

06783 89898

Press 0 for Main Menu
or a number to Continue
```

PAGE 13

```
CASTLES IN BRITAIN

SCOTLAND

Scotland boasts some
beautiful castles -
Balmoral is just one.

Phone for details

06783 89898

Press 0 for Main Menu
or a number to Continue
```

PAGE 14

```
CASTLES IN BRITAIN

WALES

41    Penholt Castle
42    Grove House
43    Coref House
44    Brioch Castle



Press 0 for Main Menu
or a number to Continue
```

PAGE 111

```
CASTLES IN BRITAIN

STANTON CASTLE

13th Century Partly
Ruined Castle

OPENING HOURS
June to September
1 pm - 5 pm
Admission £1.50/£1.00

Press 0 for Main Menu
or a number to Continue
```

PAGE 112

```
CASTLES IN BRITAIN

BRUGH CASTLE

12th Century - Recently
Renovated

OPENING HOURS
All year round
10 am - 5 pm
Admission £2 / £1

Press 0 for Main Menu
or a number to Continue
```

PAGE 113

```
CASTLES IN BRITAIN

RICARDO CASTLE

House and Grounds

OPENING HOURS
May to October
10 am - 5 pm
Admission - Free - Grounds
          - £2/£1 - House

Press 0 for Main Menu
or a number to Continue
```

PAGE 114

```
CASTLES IN BRITAIN

BLAIR HOUSE

House and Grounds

OPENING HOURS
All year round
Summer 10 am - 5 pm
Rest of year 1 pm - 5 pm
Admission - Free

Press 0 for Main Menu
or a number to Continue
```

PAGE 141

```
CASTLES IN BRITAIN

PENHOLT CASTLE

14th Century Ruins

OPENING HOURS
April to October
12 noon to 4 pm

Admission - Free

Press 0 for Main Menu
or a number to Continue
```

PAGE 142

```
CASTLES IN BRITAIN

GROVE HOUSE
19th Century House and
Gardens
OPENING HOURS
All year round
House - 1 pm to 5 pm
Gardens - 10 am to 5 pm
ADMISSION - Gardens Free
House - £2.50 / £1.50

Press 0 for Main Menu
or a number to Continue
```

PAGE 143

```
CASTLES IN BRITAIN

COREF  HOUSE

House with 19th Century
Paintings Exhibition

OPENING HOURS
All year round
10 am to 5 pm
Admission - Donation

Press 0 for Main Menu
or a number to Continue
```

PAGE 144

```
CASTLES IN BRITAIN

18th Century
More a house than a
Castle - partly ruined

OPENING HOURS
All year round
1 pm to 5 pm
Admission  £1.50

Press 0 for Main Menu
or a number to Continue
```

TREE DIAGRAM – ASSIGNMENT 2 – VIEWDATA

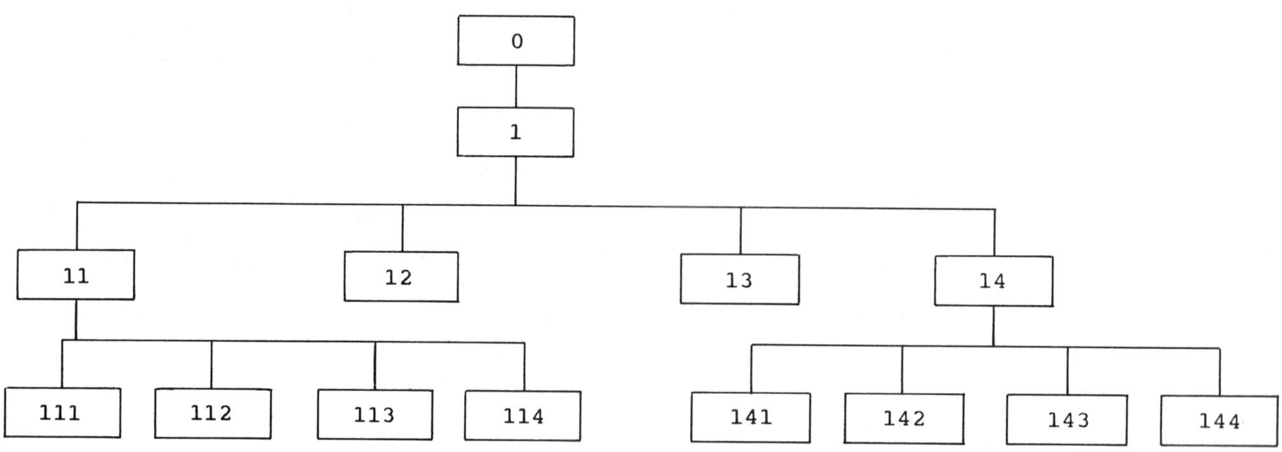

9 Desktop publishing

?

DO YOU KNOW?

How to transfer a word-processed file to ASCII format?

How to recall a drawing from the picture library?

TASK 1

1 Create the following document on a word-processing program, using the filename CASTLES.

```
CASTLES OF BRITAIN

Castle Rushen

Castle Rushen was first used as the home of the Kings of
Mann.  The last of the Norse Kings was Magnus, who died in
the castle in 1265.  It has had many uses since then, the
latest being the Civic Gaol and Lunatic Asylum for the
Island.  In 1929, it was given to the Manx nation by King
George V for services rendered in the 1914-18 war.

The main fabric of the castle is of local limestone from a
nearby quarry, and the reddish-coloured sandstone used as
flooring, window and door surrounds comes from Peel on the
West Coast.  The floors and ceilings are made of massive
slabs, some of them are 14 ft 6 in by 4 in thick.  These
came originally from Spanish Head near Port St Mary.

Peel Castle

Peel Castle stands upon St Patrick's Isle, a holy place, a
former residence of kings and the most important ancient
site in the Isle of Man.  Its architectural remains make it
one of the most remarkable fortresses in the British Isles,
for its great encircling curtain wall and its buildings,
sacred and secular, range from the 10th century through 900
years.

When Magnus Bearfoot arrived in Man in 1098 he was greatly
attracted by its fertility, in contrast with the Hebrides,
and by its military value as a jumping-off point for his
projected attack on Ireland.  He strengthened his hold on
the island by erecting forts at three strategic points.
One of them was probably St Patrick's Isle, where he also
built a residence.
```

2 Proofread, save the file and print one copy.

3 Save the file in ASCII format.

?

DO YOU KNOW?

How to draft a proposed layout?

How to put text into two columns?

How to put a heading across the page?

4 Draft a plan of the proposed layout of your document using the filename CASTLES. Put the text into two columns and a heading across the top of the page.

5 Load the desktop publishing program and create the page layout.

6 The heading BEAUTIFUL CASTLES OF BRITAIN should be centred across both columns using an appropriate style and size. Retain the ragged right margins on the columns.

7 Load the file CASTLES, and choose a reasonable type size and style.

8 Save the file and print a copy.

?

DO YOU KNOW?

How to draw a border round the heading?

How to use an image from the picture library?

9 Recall the file and make the following changes:

- place a border round the heading
- find a picture of a castle (or something representing a castle) and load it into the layout, positioning it in the centre of the layout at the end of the document.

10 Save the file and print a copy.

?

DO YOU KNOW?

How to justify text in columns?

How to draw a box?

How to change the typeface of a document?

11 Recall the file and make the following changes:

- justify the text in the columns
- draw a box measuring the width of the column by 2″ deep at the head of each column. A picture is to be inserted into each box at a later date.
- select a different typeface for the body of the document.

12 Position your name and group at the bottom of the document.

13 Save the file and print a copy.

TASK 2

1 Create the following document on a word-processing program, using the filename CAGES.

```
ANTIBIRD CAGES

Don't risk losing up to 80% of your fruit and vegetables to
the birds.

If you are a fruit and vegetable gardener, then you are no
stranger to the problems.  It is not just that the birds
have insatiable appetites - they are also extremely crafty,
watching your every move for twelve months of the year,
just waiting for the chance of a feast!  Do not be fooled
into believing that it is when the fruit are ripening that
the birds cause the most damage.  Early in the season,
seeds and buds are especially vulnerable.  It is obvious,
therefore, that you need all-the-year-round protection.
Proper protection that is designed to keep out all harmful
birds - remember that if they can ever find a flaw in your
defences, all your hope and hard work will disappear in
minutes!

ANTIBIRD CAGES are the results of years of perfecting what
was undoubtedly a very good, original cage.  The cage is
simple to erect and the frame is coated with Supergal which
is a superior form of galvanising.  A neat and functional
cage with one inch crossbars and specially designed net
hooks, ensures that there is no sagging.

The netting of the ANTIBIRD CAGE is smaller too, being made
of a three quarter inch mesh, so that no bird can enter.
The roof is a knitted netting, and the sides are of a
rough, durable rigidised netting.  There is a full seven
feet of standing room and plenty of growing area for your
produce.
```

2 Proofread, save the file and print one copy.

3 Save the file in ASCII format.

4 Draft a plan of the proposed layout of your document using the file CAGES showing the following:

- the text in two columns.
- a heading across the top of the page – PROTECT YOUR FRUIT BUSHES – FOIL THE BIRDS.
- a border around the heading.

5 Find a picture of a bird or a cage in the picture library and position this in the bottom right-hand corner of the proposed layout.

6 Put your name and group in the bottom left-hand corner of the proposed layout.

7 Load the desktop publishing program.

8 Key in the heading given above – displaying it to the best advantage using large bold headline letters.

9 Centre the heading.

10 Draw a border round this heading.

11 Load the file CAGES. Select an appropriate typeface for the text.

12 Using a different typeface and style put your name and group in the bottom left-hand corner of the page.

13 Insert the drawing you found in the bottom right-hand corner of the page.

14 Save the file and print a copy.

15 Recall the document and change the typeface and style of the body of the document.

16 Change the size of the drawing and move it to the top of the first column.

17 Save the amended file and print a copy.

Assignment 1—Desktop publishing

Section 1 – Objectives 090, 091, 092, 093, 094, 095, 096, 097, 098, 099

Section 2 – Objectives 056, 057, 059, 060, 062, 063

1 You will need the following resources:

- a desktop publishing program
- a word-processed document called BYRON
- a drawing of a man

2 Draft a plan of the layout of your document using the following:

- two columns
- a heading across the page
- a border around the heading
- indicate where the word-processed document will be positioned
- indicate where the drawing of the man will be positioned
- indicate where your name will be positioned

3 Load the desktop publishing program and create the page layout as on the plan created above.

4 For the heading 'THE BICENTENARY OF LORD BYRON'S BIRTH' use a typeface and style which will make a banner headline.

5 Centre the heading.

6 Put a border around the heading.

7 Load the ASCII-formatted, word-processed document into two columns.

8 Choose an appropriate typeface and style and justify the margins.

9 Your name should be placed at the top of the document in a different typeface and style to the rest of the text.

10 Put the drawing in the centre of the page at the bottom.

11 Save the document and print a copy.

12 Recall the document and reposition the drawing into the centre of the page beneath the heading, increasing the size.

13 Change the typeface and style of the main text of the page.

14 Save the document using the filename BYRON and print a copy.

LORD BYRON

1988 saw the bicentenary of the birth of the poet Lord Byron. Many of his readers believe that Byron was the greatest of England's poets. He was born in London on 22nd January 1788. His father left his mother almost as soon as he was born and they moved to Scotland. In 1798, at the age of 10, he succeeded to the title of 6th Baron Byron. He was educated at Harrow School and Trinity College, Cambridge.

He was very conscious of his appearance, and strove to hide his tendency to obesity by strict dieting, and by wearing trousers instead of the normal breeches, he tried to conceal the limp which was due to a malformation of the right calf and ankle.

Byron began a tour of Europe in 1807/8 and whilst on his travels started to write his famous poem 'Childe Harold'. He returned to Scotland in 1811, to the grief of the death of his mother.

Assignment 2—Desktop publishing

Section 1 – Objectives 090, 091, 092, 093, 094, 095, 096, 097, 098, 099

Section 2 – Objectives 056, 057, 059, 060, 062, 063

1 You will need the following resources:

- a desktop publishing program
- a word-processed document called PLAYERS
- a drawing of a musical note

2 Draft a plan of the layout of your document using the following:

- two columns
- a heading across the page
- a border around the heading
- indicate where the word-processed document will be positioned
- indicate where the drawing of the musical notes will be positioned
- indicate where your name will be positioned

3 Load the desktop publishing program and create the page layout as on the plan created above.

4 Key in the heading on two lines – NOTICE FOR LOCAL PRESS and WINSTON PLAYERS.

5 Centre the heading.

6 Place a decorative border around the heading.

7 Draw a box beneath the heading measuring 4″ × 3″, where a photograph will be located later.

8 Load the file PLAYERS.

9 The text is to be put into two columns with a ragged right margin for the columns. Select an appropriate typeface and style.

10 Centre your name at the bottom of the text in a different typeface and style.

11 Position three musical notes spread evenly across the bottom of the page.

12 Save the document and print a copy.

13 Recall the text and make the following changes:

- decrease the size of the musical notes
- position the additional musical notes below the box for the photograph
- change the typeface and style of the text.
- use a typeface which will make the line *Please give us your support* stand out from the remainder of the text.

14 Save the document using the filename PLAYERS and print a copy.

NOTICE FOR LOCAL PRESS

THE WINSTON PLAYERS

The Winston Players present three plays a year, a tragedy, a comedy and a musical. This year's comedy is a delightful farce by Henry Livingstone, a member of the Company. The action takes place at the stately home of 'Henry, Duke of Wessex' - the title of the play. The fun starts when his youngest daughter, Camilla, brings her fiance to meet her parents, believing that they have never met. Imagine her step-mother's surprise when she finds that the fiance, Alexander, is her lover, whom she meets once a fortnight in London. The weekend is entertaining to say the least.

Please give us your support.

The cast has been chosen from members of the Works Staff, and the costumes have been provided by James Street Costumiers. The students of the Art Department at the local College of Further Education have painted the scenery and donated their fee to a local charity of their choice. All other proceeds go to various local charities.

10 Proofreading

Proofreading is a skill which needs to be practised if it is to be accurate. A quick glance down a page is not enough to find the errors.

You may proofread from manuscript (ie handwritten) copy, typescript or printed material. Whatever the source, great care must be taken. If possible, proofread with another person.

Ask yourself the following questions:

- do I know how to spell?
- do I know basic grammar?
- do I know the rules for spacing in punctuation?

The following exercises are designed to help with proofreading. Passage A is the original text and Passage B the typed copy.

EXERCISE 1

Passage A

The windows of your home are one of the most vulnerable areas. They are exposed to extremes of weather conditions - they have to withstand the onslaught of rain, sun, frost and snow. Therefore, without regular maintenance, they can end up crumbling.

Look very carefully at your windows and decide whether it is time to repair or replace. The next decision, if replacement is the answer, is whether to install wooden surrounds or the more popular upvc which needs no further maintenance.

Passage B

The window of your home is one of the most vunerable areas. They are exposed to extremes of whether conditions-they have to withstand the onslaught of rain sun, frost and snow. Therefore, without regular maintainance, they can end up crumbeling.

Look carefully at your windows and decide weather it is time to repair or replace. The next decision, if replacement is the answer, is whether to install wooden surrounds or the more popular upvc which needs no further maintenance.

EXERCISE 2

Passage A

3175	4462	5223	6172	7474
3261	4389	5464	5816	7373
4198	4414	5317	6616	7881
8925	3987	8822	4654	3918
3191	4872	5819	6735	7257
3777	4356	5366	6324	7992

Passage B

3175	4462	5322	6172	4774
3264	4389	5464	6581	7373
3198	4144	5137	6616	7188
8925	3987	8822	4654	3918
3191	4872	5819	6735	7257
3777	4365	5633	6324	7992

EXERCISE 3

Passage A

The Plumage Act was passed in 1921. This Act was the result of pressure from groups of people who wished to put a stop to the trafficking in the feathers of wild birds. These feathers were highly valued by Victorian, and then Edwardian, milliners. The main protesters were a small group of women who banded together and called themselves the Fur and Feather Group.

Two years later, this Group became the Society for the Protection of Birds and continued to do valuable work in protecting wild birds.

Passage B

The Plumage act was passed in 1912. This Act was the result of presssure from large groups of people who wished to put a stop to the trafficing in feathers of wild birds. These feathers were highly valued by victorian, and then Edwardian, milliners. The main protestors were a small group of women who bandied together and called themselves the Fur and Feather Group.

Two years later, this Group became the society for the Protection of Birds and continued to do valuable work in protecting wild birds.

EXERCISE 4

Passage A

JUNE DIARY

June 1	11 am	Old Master Paintings
3	10 am	English and Victorian Pictures
7	2 pm	Toys, Models, Games
10	2 pm	Clocks, Watches, Barometers
12	10.30 am	Water Colours
15	11 am	Art Nouveau
21	1 pm	Nautical Equipment
27	1 pm	Textiles and Embroidery

Passage B

JUNE DAIRY

June 1	11 am	Old Master Portraits
3	10 am	English & Victorian Pictures
7	2 p.m.	Toys, models, games
10	2 pm	Clocks, Watches, Barometres
12	10.30 am	Water Colours
16	10 am	Art Nouvaeau
21	1 pm	Nauctical Equipment
27	1 pm	Textiles and Embriodery

EXERCISE 5

Passage A

MICROWAVE OVENS

A microwave oven will make your life easier. It cooks in a similar way to a little broadcasting station. Inside the oven is a special power source called a MAGNETRON TUBE. When activated by electricity, the tube produces short high-frequency waves which are similar to radio waves. As these waves will not penetrate metal, it is important to use dishes, plates, etc which are designed for use in a microwave.

Passage B

<u>Microwave Ovens</u>

A microwave oven will make your life easer. It is more than an oven. It cooks in a similar way to a little broadcasting station. Inside the oven is a special power sauce called a magneton tube. When activated by electricity the tube produces short high - frequency waves which are simalar to radio waves. As these waves will not penetrate metal, it is improtant to use dishes, plates etc which are designed for use in a microwave.

EXERCISE 6

Passage A

The cleaning lady came to me the other day and asked if it was possible for her to catch this 'computer virus' she had heard about.

What is this virus and what does it do? The virus is, in fact, a program which can alter the information stored on the computer by attaching itself to the very nerve centre of your system - the computer code. This program can wipe out files or make a screenful of information disappear before your eyes. There are now several anti-virus packages which are available to remove the virus.

Passage B

```
The cleaneing lady came to me the other day and asked if it was
posible for her to catch this ' computer virus ' she had heard
about.

What is this virus and what does it do?  The virus is in fact, a
programme which can alter the infromation stored on the computer
by attaching itself to the nerve centre of your system- the
computor code.  This program can wipe out files or make a screen
of information disappear before your eyes.  There are now several
anti - virus packages which are available to remove the virus.
```

EXERCISE 7

Passage A

MODEL	PRICE	ZOOM	APERTURE
P279	625	8:1	F1.2
KL101	615	12:1	F1.4
KL256	900	6:1	F1.6
KL100	719	12:1	F1.2
KL110	890	10:1	F1.4
P511	799	10:1	F1.2
P716	650	8:1	F1.4
P331	699	6:1	F1.6
T216	810	10:1	F1.6

Passage B

MODEL	PRICE	ZOOM	APERTURE
PP279	625	8:1	F1.2
KL101	651	2:1	F1.4
KL526	990	6:1	F1.6
Kl100	719	12:1	f1.2
KL110	990	10:1	F1.4
P511	799	12:1	F1.6
PP16	650	18:1	F1.4
P331	599	16:1	F1.4
TP216	810	12:1	F1.6

EXERCISE 8

Passage A

Make/Model		cc	kw	Tow Limit
Prince	T136	998	12.3	8.0
	T216	1275	15.9	18.7
	T321	1598	19.1	22.6
	T455	1994	26.3	30.5
Princess	P171	1392	17.2	17.7
	P271	1608	18.6	17.7
	P371	1993	20.9	26.5

Passage B

Make/Model		c.c.	kw	Tow limit
Prince	T136	989	12.3	8.0
	T261	1275	15.8	18.7
	T321	1598	19.1	21.6
	T455	1499	26.3	30.5
Princess	P171	1392	17.7	17.7
	P217	1608	18.6	17.9
	P371	1993	20.9	26.5

EXERCISE 9

Passage A

SCOTTISH BROCHS

What is a broch? It is a fortified round tower built in Scotland in Roman times. Archaeologists believe that five hundred of them were built by the local communities throughout the north and west of the country. They were built to an identical pattern, miles apart, when transport and travel was very difficult.

Who built them and why? They were built in areas easy to defend and were very large. The largest brochs were over eighty feet in diameter and in height, with very thick walls. Beneath them were a maze of passages and staircases.

Passage B

Scottish Brochs

What is a broch. It is a fortified round-tower built in Scotland in Roman times. Archaeoalogists believe that 500 of them were built by the local commmunities throughout the north and west of the country. They were built to an identicle pattern, miles apart when transport and travel was very difficult.

Who built them and why? They were built in areas easy to defend and were very large. The largest brochs were over eighty feet in diametre and in height, with thick walls. Beneath them were a mase of passages and staircases.

Appendix

Profile sentences from the CLAIT syllabus

CLAIT is the examination provided by the Royal Society of Arts to test the knowledge of candidates on a variety of software packages. The assignments which must be undertaken are assessed in two sections:

SECTION 1 Applications of Computers and Information Technology; and

SECTION 2 Computers and Information Technology

Each component is divided into a number of profile sentences which must be carried out by the student. If all sentences are carried out correctly, the student is given a Pass in that application and is awarded a certificate on the following basis:

Less than 3 Applications – Profile Certificate
3 or more Applications – RSA Stage I Certificate

A number of these sentences are 'starred'. If these are carried out accurately, the student is awarded the RSA Stage I Certificate with Distinction.

SECTION 1

(a)	WORD PROCESSING		
01	ENTER text	P1	Enter, load and save text
02	LOAD text		
03	SAVE text		
04	INSERT words	P2	Insert/delete/replace words;
05	INSERT paragraph		Insert/delete paragraphs
06	DELETE words		
07	DELETE paragraph		
08	REPLACE words		
09	CHANGE margins	P3	Change margins
	FORMAT printout:	*P4	Change layout
010*	line-spacing		
011*	justification on/off		
(b)	SPREADSHEETS		
012	ENTER text	P5	Enter and edit text and numeric data
013	ENTER numeric data		
014	DELETE entries		
015	REPLACE entries		
016	REPLICATE entries	P6	Replicate in a spreadsheet
017	CHANGE the format	P7	Change the format
018	USE a formula	P8	Use formulae

019*	ADD a row or column	*P9	Extend the spreadsheet
020*	PROJECT new values		
(c)	DATABASE		
021	SET UP files containing alphabetic and numeric fields within the record	P10	Set up a database
022	ENTER data	P11	Enter data and edit the database
023	ADD records		
024	DELETE records		
025	EDIT records		
026	SORT records by a keyfield	P12	Formulate selection procedures for target records
027	SEARCH records by a keyfield		
028*	PRINT selected fields	*P13	Print selected fields
029*	SEARCH on more than one criterion	*P14	Search on more than one criterion
(d)	VIDEOTEX SYSTEMS		
030	LOG ON to a viewdata and/or teletext system	P15	Log on to videotext system
031	TRACE pages on a specific topic	P16	Trace pages on a specific topic
032	AMEND a directory of pages available	P17	Amend a directory of pages available
033	EDIT a page	P18	Edit a page
034	CHANGE THE ROUTEING of a page	P19	Change the routeing of a page
	COMPOSE a new page using techniques of:	*P20	Compose a new page using a variety of techniques
035*	coloured text		
036*	double height characters		
037*	flashing		
038*	graphics		
039*	background filling		
(e)	BUSINESS/ACCOUNTING PACKAGES		STOCK CONTROL/PAYROLL
040	ENTER a variety of business information relevant to the package	P21	Enter information
041	SEARCH the package for information	P22	Search the package for information
042	ADD records	P23	Change file details
043	DELETE records		
044	CHANGE records		
045*	PRODUCE a report on specified information	*P24	Produce a report on specified information
(f)	GRAPHICS/PLOTTING		
	Drawing System		
046	DRAW shapes/symbols	P25	Draw, change, label and store shapes/symbols
047	CHANGE shapes/symbols		

048	STORE shapes/symbols		
049	COLOUR or SHADE sections		
050	USE text to label drawings		
	Graphical Representation		
	USE a variety of prepared data to produce:	P26	Produce graphical outputs from numeric data
051	pie charts		
052	histograms		
053	graphs		
054	USE text to label graphs/charts		
055*	USE a formula to produce a graph	*P27	Use a formula to produce a graph
	DESKTOP PUBLISHING (pilot)		
090	PLAN layout incorporating columns and a page wide heading from given materials	P50	Plan layout
091	LOAD previously prepared text	P51	Use previously prepared text and images
092	USE previously prepared images		
093	INPUT text		
094	CENTRE text		
095	JUSTIFY text		
096	USE a minimum of 3 type sizes and 2 type styles	P53	Use a range of text styles and sizes
097	DRAW borders or a box	P54	Use simple border facilities
098*	USE serif and sans-serif typefaces	*P55	Change the presentation
099*	ADJUST the image		

SECTION 2

(a)	USING THE COMPUTER SYSTEM		
056	POWER UP in correct sequence	P28	Start up a computer system; load the program and data; close dcwn the system
057	LOAD a program		
058	LOAD data into the system		
059	CLOSE DOWN the system in correct sequence		
(b)	USING COMPONENTS OF COMPUTER SYSTEM		
(i)	*Input Device*		
060	USE the keyboard or other input device to enter data	P29	Use an input device
(ii)	*Output Device*		
	Use the printer to output information	P30	Use a printer
061	LOAD paper into printer, set paper and printer to the top of a form		
062	CHECK printer is on-line		
063	OUTPUT hard copy		

(iii)	*Storage*		
Either			
064	FORMAT a blank disk or select an empty user area	P31	Use a disk storage system
065	COPY a file from one disk to another or copy a file from one user area to another		
066	LIST the directory of files available		
067	DELETE a file from disk or user area		
or		*or*	
068	LOAD a file from tape	P32	Use a tape storage system
069	SAVE a program on tape		
070	OPERATE a simple system to ensure the backing up of data	P33	Operate a simple system to ensure the backing up of data
(c)	USING A COMPUTER AS A COMMUNICATING DEVICE		
071	CONNECT the computer, using appropriate hardware and software to: (a) send information to, or (b) receive or retrieve information from, another source (eg another computer) locally through a network or remotely through an external communications system	P34	Use a computer as a communicating device